AUDIO IN ADVERTISING

Also by Dick Weissman

The Music Business: Career Opportunities and Self-Defense
The Folk Music Sourcebook (with Larry Sandberg)

AUDIO IN ADVERTISING

Ron Lockhart and Dick Weissman

A PRACTICAL GUIDE TO PRODUCING AND RECORDING MUSIC, VOICEOVERS, AND SOUND EFFECTS

FREDERICK UNGAR PUBLISHING CO.
New York

Copyright © 1982 by Ron Lockhart and Dick Weissman
Printed in the United States of America
Design by Anita Duncan

Library of Congress Cataloging in Publication Data

Lockhart, Ron.
   Audio in advertising.

   Bibliography: p.
   Includes index.
   1. Sound recording industry.   2. Radio advertising.   3. Television
advertising.   I. Weissman, Dick.   II. Title.

ML3790.L6   621.389'3   81-40467
ISBN 0-8044-5607-0   AACR2

Acknowledgments

The knowledge that I have picked up over the years has been due in large part to a group of people who had faith in my abilities and talent, and made sure that I learned what I needed to know. There are few chances to publicly acknowledge their contribution to my career, so I would like to do so now.

To Mitch Leigh, who gave me my first chance to work on commercials. To Herman Edel who forgave a lot of mistakes and to his producer Susan Hamilton, who is not only an outstanding musician but one of the most savvy producers I have ever met. To the late Betsy Cohen of CBS who gave me a chance to develop my skills in the best studios in the world while having the time of my life. To all of you, a very grateful "thank you."

RON LOCKHART

New York City, NY

Most of my knowledge of recording studio procedures was learned under the guidance of a brilliant engineer named Bill Schwartau. He was the first engineer that I met who used the equipment in the studio as a vehicle to produce musical and emotional effects, and he was never intimidated by technical matters. I would also like to thank Jerome Gilmer, a composer and arranger in Denver, for his reactions to some of the material in this book.

DICK WEISSMAN

Boulder, Colorado

Both authors would like to thank the following people for their invaluable assistance in writing this book. Without it, this project would never have reached fruition. Jane Z. Paisley, Jerry Holland, Jim McCurdy, Pat Whitaker, Bobby Schaffner, John Quinn and The Mix Place, Bill Blachly, Stu Gellman, George Klabin and Sound Ideas Recording Studios, Steve Karmen, Stan Kahan, Gaye Cooper, Kathy Holt, Gary Cumiskey, Ampex Corporation and MCI Corporation, Bobbie Smallheiser, First Edition Editing, Inc., Tony Siggia and Philip Winsor.

All photos by Gary Cumiskey except where noted.

All illustrations by Gaye Cooper and Kathy Holt of Cooper-Holt Design, Inc.

v

Contents

Foreword

The insistent, persuasive power of advertising is a tremendous force. Day and night, and on every radio and television station, the consumer is subjected to the mind-tempting techniques of Madison Avenue, gently reminding that a sponsor is providing the entertainment by offering something for sale through advertising. Effective advertising is the gateway to the market place of the world.

Advertising music is the most distinctive, purposeful music art form. No spoken word or visual image communicates with the instant recognition of a catchy jingle, and no background score has more lasting social and psychological impact than the underscore for a commercial.

In clear, concise language, AUDIO IN ADVERTISING provides a step-by-step guide to understanding the production of a successful advertising soundtrack. Here, the mysteries of audio are explained for the benefit of professionals as well as newcomers to the field.

Ron Lockhart and Dick Weissman have written the first easy-to-read description of the inner workings of the world of musical advertising.

AUDIO IN ADVERTISING is recommended to agency producers, students of advertising, and to every person concerned with the musical messages that cannot be denied.

Steve Karmen

Preface

This book is designed to teach you what goes on in the studio, so that you can operate to your fullest potential, no matter what your background. More than that, it is designed to help you have fun in the studio. The first time you step into a large recording complex can be a frightening experience. There is usually a good reason when you are in a studio in the first place—you may be a copywriter, producer, music supervisor, or the talent that will sing, play, or announce on the commercial. The two of us have collected some reasonably colorful horror stories over the years, tales that involve nervousness, incompetence, equipment failures, and the like. Modern recording is a very enjoyable and satisfying experience, and working with the best musicians and singers in the country, (the very same ones who make hit records when they are not doing jingles), is a head trip in itself. Provided that you go into the studio knowing that your jingle or copy is *really* ready to record, and that your budget has purchased the best possible talent, it's hard to match the satisfaction gained from working in the contemporary recording studios.

New York is considered by most people to be the center of recording for radio and television commercials; and in New York, as well as other major recording centers (Los Angeles, Nashville, Chicago, and Montreal), lives the best and most versatile talent in the world. The actors and actresses who perform your copy can create almost anything you can imagine, and the musicians and singers are also unmatched. The larger studios in these cities contain millions of dollars worth of sophisticated recording equipment that has all been designed to help you make what you are recording sound as good as possible.

Our goal is to show you what these talented people can do in the studio, how best to work with them, and how to use the multitude of equipment that today's recording environment offers.

You don't need to be an engineer or producer to get the sound you want in the studio; instead, you need to have the same basic understanding of the recording process that enables you to use your home stereo. The average person can't repair a sophisticated automobile, but anyone with a license can drive the beast.

Our approach is to explain the recording process step by step, in nontechnical language that the lay person can follow. We are also including pictures and diagrams of the equipment that you will find in most of today's

1

studios. The first part of this book focuses on the recording studio, what the equipment is, how it works, and how you can best use it. The next time you're in the studio, check out all of those knobs and buttons. Don't feel intimidated! You are the client and you are paying a high price to get a finished product that will suit your needs. Don't be ashamed to ask for a playback of a tape at a louder or softer level. If something doesn't seem to be working, ask the producer or engineer why an instrument or a particular microphone sounds the way it does. They are there to serve you, and if they don't, you ought to take your business elsewhere.

The second section of the book deals with the way that sound and picture work together; the advantages or differences between them, working with film or videotape (as regards audio); how to combine music, dialogue, and sound effects and how to do basic film and videotape mathematics. We explain how careful pre-production can save you valuable time, money, and aggravation, and we discuss some of the problems in making picture and sound work together.

We end with a section on the uses of music in advertising. This includes an explanation of how music can help you sell a product, some thoughts about lyrics and tunes that sell, and an appendix (with examples) that breaks down contemporary musical styles into various categories. A glossary is included that explains all of the fancy technical terms like "full coat," "stripe," "leakage," and all of those other ten-dollar words that engineers, music producers, and film editors love to throw around.

Most of all, we want you to enjoy and understand this book. It is designed to help you, based on our experiences as composers, arrangers, musicians, singers, and producers with a combined total of over thirty-five years of studio experience. We get old just thinking about it!

PART ONE

The Contemporary Recording Studio

Pre-Production and Focus

Before we examine the recording studio itself, we need to discuss some of the pre-production work that will make your life in the studio productive and easy. Probably the biggest single mistake that all advertising personnel and suppliers make is to underestimate the value of pre-production. Your studio time should be devoted to the execution of your creative ideas and not wasted in figuring out how to correct your timings and copy (the written text). If there is one major error that occurs over and over again it is the lack of pre-production.

Let's say that you are working on a project, maybe a new kind of chocolate bar. First, keep in mind (if you decided that you want to use music to tell your message) that music is most effective when it focuses on one point. While copy can tell any story you can think of, music becomes less effective as the lyrics get more complicated. Using the example above, and assuming that you have decided to use music to tell your story, try to figure out what the single most important product difference might be that you would want to emphasize. You may decide that the fact that the chocolate is *crunchy* is the selling point to hone in on. The price, color of the wrapper, and the size of the candy bar are not the most important things to stress at this time. Here is a great example of how this process works:

A few years ago McDonald's ran a campaign for their Big Mac sandwich. They decided to focus attention on the sandwich itself. What they created was a lyric that was packed with words: "two all-beef patties, special sauce, lettuce, cheese, pickles, onions, on a sesame-seed bun." But that still focused on only *one* product point, the sandwich. Price, cleanliness of the store, french fries, and other copy points were not touched on, so that while the commercial may appear to be covering a great many items it is in reality discussing only one product point. Clever!

The next thing you need is a music house to write your music for this new chocolate bar. In this book we use the terms "music house," "music producer," and "composer-arranger" interchangeably. Working with most music houses will involve using the services of several people who fulfill these various jobs. You must also decide whether the lyric will come from the advertising agency or whether you will assign the job to a music house. At this point we should be quite honest with you about another common mistake. *Most* copywriters are not lyricists. They write advertising copy better than anyone, and understand the needs of their client far better than a music producer or composer; but they are usually not conversant enough with the very special art of writing lyrics.

A person who is accustomed to creating song lyrics has a good idea of the relationship between lyric and melody. He knows from past experience what will "sing" and what will not. If you're *not* one of these people, don't write a finished lyric. By all means come into a meeting with your prospective supplier(s) with the key words (in our example, *crunchy*), and concepts and slogans that you feel are necessary to make your commercial work.

If you are not going to write the lyric, then who will? Listen to the demo reels that every music house uses to demonstrate its best or latest work. They will be happy (thrilled might be a better word) to give you a current sample reel and to keep you on their mailing list. Look for a music house that has a jingle in the same general vein as the one you imagine for your new chocolate bar. Are the lyrics good, brilliant, acceptable, or terrible? If you like the lyrics, ask who wrote them. Was it the agency where the work originated, or was it a lyricist hired by the music house? In the end, it may well be that the lyrics were a joint effort. You will be there to make sure that the major points are stressed and that the lyricist doesn't write something so awkward, ungrammatical, or obscure that it embarrasses you or the agency. No matter who writes the lyric, make sure that the agency and you have the final approval of the lyric *before* you go into the recording session. (Remember, pre-production!)

In Robert Townsend's book, *Up the Organization,* he stressed that one of the keys to working in advertising is the ability to delegate authority. Your music house should be rewarded if its productions succeed and fired if they show poorly in the marketplace. If the agency hamstrings the music house with poor lyrics, it's difficult to place the blame on them when a campaign falls flat.

Next, listen to the sample reels to see which music house has music that appeals to your tastes. Usually, you'll recognize a piece of music from having heard it on the air. A composition that has been on the air for a long time is obviously effective, and that also should be something you consider in your choice. If you can't find any sample reel that has a piece of music that is just what you're looking for, choose the best two or three and ask the music houses to do a **demo** for your new chocolate bar. A demo is a demonstration tape of the melody and lyric that has been composed for you (in general, any demonstration tape). You will probably be expected to pay a submission fee to each music house in compensation for their think time, but then you can choose from the best compositions submitted to you.

If you find a music reel that has just the type of music that you've been "hearing," that should be the clear choice for the music house you work with on your job. However, make sure, when you contact them, that you explain what piece of music attracted you to them. This will insure that if the music house uses several different composers and arrangers, your job will be assigned to the one who wrote the composition you liked.

Tell your music house everything that you can about the product, including whether the jingle will be used on radio *and* TV or only on one of the two, the length of the "spot" (commercial), i.e. :30, :60, and anything else that you consider pertinent. It is better to give too much information than not to give enough. The music house will discard whatever information is superfluous. Certainly don't forget to tell them that *crunchy* is the password for the day and the central concept you have decided to pursue.

Within a few days you will receive your first demo tapes. They usually contain a solo voice and a piano or guitar accompaniment, but that is enough to give you a general idea of what the composer and lyricist have in mind. However, make sure that you fully understand what is going to happen at the recording session. A good music house should be able to give you an accurate idea of what the final product is going to be. This includes everything from budget to orchestration.

If you have chosen two or more houses, this is the time to narrow it down to one. Call the others and tell them "thanks but no thanks." This is a simple courtesy that is often overlooked. Sooner or later an experienced producer works with every supplier, and it is amazing how slowly old wounds heal. A little courtesy goes a long way in your career.

Now ask your chosen music supplier to elaborate on their composition so that you have a crystal-clear idea of what you are going to get inside the recording studio. The first thing to do is explain all the changes that you'd like to make, recheck your timings, and then ask them to redo the demo. Perhaps it would be wise, if this is early in your career and one of your first times in the recording studio, to ask the music house to use a synthesizer to simulate the sound of some of the instruments. Synthesizers can imitate anything from strings and brass to drums and other percussion. You may have to pay a small fee to have this done (remember that your composer and producer are spending a lot of time for which they still have received no real compensation), but this makes for a predictable recording session. Also, you will almost surely need to play this music for your client for final approval (both creative and financial). Your client is not a musician, copywriter, or agency producer. The closer a demo comes to sounding like the finished product, the more intelligent a judgment the client can make as to whether the commercial is appropriate for the product. If you take a simple demo of guitar and voice or piano and voice to your client and say, "the strings will go here and the brass will go there," or that the music will accomplish this or that, he probably isn't going to know what you are talking about. If it is necessary to bolster your client's confidence regarding the demo, why not play him the sample reel of the music house you have chosen. This will assure him that he is working with an experienced supplier, and that while he may not understand everything about music, he will be confident that the music supplied will be top-notch.

On your part, good pre-production includes having *all* your timings worked out before you go into studio. An absolute no-no is informing the arranger and/or composer in the studio, "Uh, Ron, we decided to do another :20 version. That won't be any trouble, will it?"

Not only will it be a lot of trouble, it is extremely wasteful. At $200 an hour or more for studio time, and talent costs being as high as they are, it is wise *not* to pull surprises in the studio.

Timings

Remember that written copy is going to produce different timings when mumbled in your office than when a singer actually performs it or an announcer actually reads it. For example, if you are doing a soul or new-wave version of our "Crunchies" jingle, you might have a lyric reading:

> I really want you all to know
> You'll love those chocolate Crunchies so

The composer might phrase it:

> I really, really want you to know-o-o
> You're going to love, really love
> Those Crunchies so-o-o

Also, while it only takes about :04 to read this lyric in a sing-song type voice, music is usually slower paced. By the time you allow for extra *beats* for the music and allow for tempo differences, a pretty good bet is that the lyric will take *twice* as long to sing as it does to speak. Therefore, our example above, which took us :04 to read, should be timed allowing :08 to sing.

Another common goof is to time copy while mumbling it into your shirt. Read your copy *aloud* to see if it is easy to read, can be read at the pace you "hear," still be understandable, and fit into your timing requirements. One of the most frustrating things that can happen at a voiceover recording session is to have :35 worth of copy for a :30 spot. All of these problems can be avoided with a little pre-production!

Choosing the Recording Studio

Choosing the studio is a simple matter. The music producer you have hired will choose the studio based on your needs and his budgetary limitations. You have nothing more to do than to show up at the session. If you are experienced at recording and have been in several different studios, you might find that you prefer one over another. Simply tell your music producer which one you like. If *you* are the one doing the renting of the studio, size up your needs before you book a facility. For instance, do you need projection equipment so that you can play back your recording to the film that you have already shot? You may have a special effect that you want on a voice and you might be unfamiliar with the studio equipment that will produce that effect.

For most voiceover recordings a monaural tape recorder is just fine. A voiceover recording is a recording made with only an announcer (or announcers). Sometimes the announcer reads the copy while listening to the music track. At other times only a stopwatch is used to assure that the copy runs to the correct time and will fit in the section you have allowed for copy. (This section is often called a "donut".) Obviously, if you have a large music session you will need a sophisticated studio. There are many fine studios, however, that specialize in doing only voiceovers. They may not have 24-track tape recorders, but they offer the right equipment for the job. If you have already finished your music recording session and have a final mono tape of it and want the announcer to read the copy while hearing your jingle, you can easily get away with one of the smaller studios.

The price and availability of the studio are always factors to consider in your choice, but the ultimate decision should be based on the engineer you will be using. As in photography, where the person behind the camera is more important than the camera itself, the man or woman behind the recording **console** is far more important than the equipment itself. A great engineer can make a mediocre studio the right place for your jingle. On the other hand, a studio with the latest in gadgetry and machines is of absolutely no value to you if the engineer is not able to get the sound you want.

As a child, Dick Weissman had an experience that shows how a great craftsperson works capably with inferior tools. He saw Larry Adler, the harmonica virtuoso, do a children's concert with the Philadelphia Orchestra. Adler had lost his harmonica and appealed to the audience to see if some child happened to bring one with him. He proceeded to play a brilliant concert with a borrowed twenty-five-cent harmonica. It is not the equipment that is crucial but the mastery of the engineer over that equipment. A good engineer is patient, creative, flexible, knows the equipment and can operate it quickly, and can concentrate under pressure despite distractions.

Pre-Score and Post-Score

The term "pre-score" is used to describe music recorded *before* you shoot your commercial on film or videotape. "Post-score" is a term applied to music that is recorded *after* you are finished with the filming or taping.

A pre-score situation would occur when the actors have to be in "sync" (synchronized) with the sound track. As an example, the popular Doctor Pepper television commercials are pre-scored. The actors and actresses have to move their lips in time with the music to give the illusion that they are singing while they are performing **on-camera.** Unfortunately, no one has yet figured out a way to record **live** (on a set) that captures the fidelity available in a recording studio. Part of the problem is also financial. An orchestra would have to be paid to sit and play the music over and over again even if their performance was perfect because a **shot** was lost or a dancer slipped. It is much easier to pre-record (pre-score) the music and simply play it back while the cameras are rolling. There is a process that keeps everything synchronized so the illusion is that it's all happening live, and we'll describe that later.

An example of post-scoring a commercial would be when it was unnecessary for the actors or director to synchronize with the sound track. If the music and lyrics serve as a background accompaniment then there is no need for the playback of the sound track on the set. Or, if there are no lyrics and the music is intended to be in the background to enhance the commercial, there is generally no need to pre-score.

As a general rule of thumb, anything requiring *"lip-sync"* (the actors and actresses moving their mouths as if they were actually singing) requires a pre-score. Anything *not* requiring lip-sync is usually a post-score.

If a composer and/or arranger can view the film after it has been shot and roughly put together by a film editor, they will have a better idea of just what your particular commercial needs. They can get a feel for the pace the art director had in mind when he conceived the commercial and give you the music to match.

Sometimes a film editor prefers pre-scoring even if it is not necessary to the shooting of the spot. This is because he gets a feel for the spot by listening to the music and lyrics and can get a pace that he can **cut** the commercial to.

There is nothing wrong with *either* method and during your career you will certainly be required to do both. Again, good pre-production is the key to figuring out your needs. Call a meeting with your film editor, director, and music producer and discuss it with them. They will be impressed with your professionalism for conferring with them on this decision.

A Brief History of the Recording Studio

Before we describe that space-age toy, the recording studio, a brief historical discussion is in order.

Tape recorders first appeared on the scene right after World War II. The first professional tape recorders were monaural, or one-track machines. (In other words, there was no stereo). Since there was only one **track**, it was not possible, as it is today, to record the musicians at one time and the singers at another. All music was recorded live, along with the announcer copy, and any instrumental solos. What you heard was what you got. If a big band, an announcer, and singers were used on a large recording session, everything had to be recorded simultaneously! All decisions had to be made at the time of recording by the music producer and agency representative. If any element went wrong, the whole **take** had to be redone. If it was decided after everyone left the studio that they liked everything but the announcer, or that copy had to be changed, *everyone* had to be recalled to re-record the entire commercial. That helps to explain why so much announcer copy was done live in the early days of radio and TV.

In the early 1950s, as the technology of tape became more accepted, a process known as "overdubbing" came into use. Overdubbing was a way of adding a singer or instrumental solo *after* the basic music track had already been recorded and the orchestra sent home. Here, briefly, is how it worked. A studio had two monaural tape recorders. On machine #1 the engineer recorded the orchestra. After everyone approved that recording, a connection was made from machine #1 to machine #2 through the recording console. Then the singer or instrumentalist would go into the studio and stand in front of a microphone that was also connected into the console. The overdubbing process was ready to begin.

The tape on machine #1 was rewound to the beginning. Then, as machine #1 was being played back, it was also being recorded on machine #2. In other words, it was making a **tape copy.** But at the same time that the tape was being **copied,** the singer was listening to the playback of machine #1 through his or her earphones and singing or playing into the microphone in time to the music. This was also being sent to, and recorded on, machine

#2, which created a composite. The balance between the singer or instrumentalist and the orchestra was controlled by the engineer on the console. The result was an overdubbed (composite) recording of the original orchestra and one added element. The recording could be done over and over until you got a satisfactory performance. The number of elements you could overdub, however, was limited, since the sound quality started to suffer after the third or fourth time. Each successive overdub is called a new **generation** and each generation has less sound quality than the preceding generation. It is like making a copy of your favorite photograph from the photograph and not the negative. The quality starts to deteriorate.

By the early 1960s stereo sound had appeared. The advances in electronics and tape technology allowed for two-track, three-track, and eventually four-track tape recorders. Now, instead of going through the cumbersome process that we described above, a machine with four tracks was used to accomplish the same thing! The orchestra could be recorded on track one, the instrumental soloist on track two, the singer on track three, and the announcer on track four. Fancy electronics kept the whole thing synchronized and the term "selective-synchronization," or "sel-sync" for short, was born. Sel-sync was the term used for overdubbing an additional element to the band. To explain further how all this works we need to explain a bit about the way professional tape recorders are designed.

Professional tape recorders have three heads (see diagram 1). Head number one is the erase head. It simply erases whatever is on the tape when the machine is in the "record" mode and cannot be turned on or off by the engineer. If the tape is blank and the machine is put into "record" the erase head still erases.

Next in line is the record head, and it does exactly what the name implies: record. Under *very special circumstances*, which we will explain shortly, the record head can occasionally be a playback head. For now, just remember that the record head is the head that does the recording.

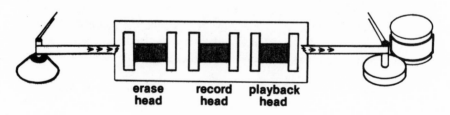

**erase   record   playback
head   head   head**

A typical head assembly

Diagram 1

A typical two-track head assembly. *Ampex Corporation*

A typical 24-track head assembly. *Ampex Corporation*

The last head is the playback head, and it has one job only: playback of whatever has been recorded on the tape. It is designed to give back all of the fidelity that was recorded on the tape by the record head. Albeit important, this is the playback head's *only* function.

Today, tape recorders have grown up. We now have 24-track tape recorders as standard equipment, and many of the more sophisticated facilities are installing 32-track equipment. Simply stated, a 24-track recorder in the eighties would be comparable to having twenty-four monaural machines in the fifties. What a difference!

There are still applications, and essential ones at that, for machines smaller than 24 tracks. For instance, the old mono machine is still used to create the final master tape that consists of all the 24 tracks **mixed down** to one. Two-track is used in the record industry to create stereo masters (and in advertising to create stereo mixes for FM radio), and four-track to create something called a "full coat," which we will discuss in part two of this book. Today's well-equipped studio has *all* of these machines and usually a whole lot more.

This brings us to the workings of the contemporary recording studio. Today, we have the ability to record our Crunchies jingle using all 24 tracks of the tape recorder. If our recording session consisted of 22 musicians, one singer, and one announcer, we would in theory use all 24 tracks on the machine. But often a single instrument, such as a drum set that consists of several different sounds, is recorded on a number of separate tracks. The bass drum, snare drum, tom-toms, and cymbals all represent different sounds that should be **miked** separately (a different microphone on each drum) and recorded on separate tracks. Therefore, an engineer might decide to devote 4 tracks to the drums alone. In this way he can make any part of the drum set, say the snare drum, louder or softer to give the drums a totally different **feel**.

The opposite of that example would be the recording of the violins. While a music arranger might require 10 violin players to perform the music he or she has written, the engineer will only use one track to record them. Only if the violins were playing in **harmony** (playing several different notes at the same time) would an engineer consider **splitting** them onto different tracks.

One potential problem in **multi-track recording** is what is known as **leakage**. Leakage occurs when material recorded on one microphone leaks over to another microphone. If we have an acoustic guitar player seated next to the drummer, the sound of the drums will surely be picked up on the guitar microphone because of the tremendous difference in the volume of these two instruments. The problem occurs when we want to **mix** (finalize) the tape and bring up the guitar to make it louder. Every time we bring up the guitar we

A two-track tape recorder
Ampex Corporation

A four-track tape recorder.
Ampex Corporation

A 24-track tape recorder.
Ampex Corporation

also bring up the drums. For this reason wooden baffles and isolation booths are set up in the studio to limit the amount of leakage from one mike to another. The engineer listens to each track to make sure the amount of leakage is either minimal or nonexistent. This listening is done in the control room, which is separated from the room where the actual recording takes place by a thick, soundproof piece of glass. The engineer can *see* what is happening while he *hears* what is going on over the speakers in the control room.

Bouncing

Sometimes a commercial has so many different elements that even twenty-four tracks may not be enough. When this happens we can *combine* already recorded tracks by using a process called "bouncing." Let's say that we have used up twenty-two of our twenty-four tracks but we still have several parts to record. We need to open up additional room on the tape to accomplish this. The engineer looks at the "track sheet" (see diagrams 2 and 3), a sheet that indicates what instruments or voices are on each track, and sees that he recorded the woodwinds on three separate tracks: 16, 17, and 18. He may combine those three woodwind tracks (mix them, so to speak) and send them to track 23, which is one of our open and as yet unused tracks.

The engineer balances all of the woodwinds so that he and the music producer are satisfied with the sound. He rewinds the machine to the beginning of the music and instructs the tape recorder to take this combined sound and record (bounce) it onto track 23. After the tape has run through to the end of the music, tracks 16, 17, and 18 are available for recording. Since all of the woodwinds have been combined and sent to a different track, the engineer is now free to *erase* tracks 16, 17 and 18 and record new material there. Instead of only two available tracks for recording we have four (16, 17, 18, and 22). If we need even more room to record, we can continue to combine tracks and bounce them over to an unused track and create even more room.

There are important things to remember about bouncing. You *must* have at least one available track to start bouncing. If there are no available tracks you will have to erase a track to create more room.

Once the tracks are bounced (combined and transferred) the relationship of one instrument to another is locked into balance on that track and cannot be changed. Listen carefully to each **pass** (attempt) made at bouncing, and unless you are absolutely satisfied with the way the combined instruments sound, redo it. In our example above, the relative balances of the woodwinds cannot be changed once the bouncing process is completed, i.e. after you have *erased* the woodwind tracks.

Title:			Count #		Reel #		Take #
CLICK TRACK 11-0 ¹	DRUMS (snare) ²	DRUMS (foot pedal) ³	DRUMS (cymbals) ⁴	PIANO (treble) ⁵	PIANO (bass) ⁶	ELECTRIC BASS ⁷	ELECTRIC GUITAR ⁸
Acoustic Guitar ⁹	Violins ¹⁰	Violins ¹¹	Viola ¹²	Celli ¹³	Synthe-sizer ¹⁴	Saxophone ¹⁵	Flutes ¹⁶
Oboe ¹⁷	Clarinet ¹⁸	Trumpets ¹⁹	Trombones ²⁰	French Horns ²¹	²²	²³	60 Cycle Sync. ²⁴

Available tracks BEFORE the "bounce".

Diagram 2

Title:			Count #		Reel #		Take #
CLICK TRACK 11-0 ¹	DRUMS (snare) ²	DRUMS (foot pedal) ³	DRUMS (cymbal) ⁴	PIANO (treble) ⁵	PIANO (bass) ⁶	ELECTRIC BASS ⁷	ELECTRIC GUITAR ⁸
Acoustic Guitar ⁹	Violins ¹⁰	Violins ¹¹	Viola ¹²	Celli ¹³	Synthe-sizer ¹⁴	Saxophone ¹⁵	¹⁶
¹⁷	¹⁸	Trumpets ¹⁹	Trombones ²⁰	French Horns ²¹	²²	Flutes, Oboe & Clarinet ²³	60 cycle Sync. ²⁴

Available tracks AFTER the "bounce".

Diagram 3

Sel-Synchronization

This is a good time to get one of those technical facts out of the way. You may have been wondering why bouncing works. After all, the record head is separated from the playback head on the tape recorder by an inch or two. How does it all stay in "sync"? Truly, this is the magic of electronics.

Remember a little while ago we said that the record head under *very special circumstances* can also be a playback head? This is one of those very special circumstances. The record head will act like a playback head *except* on the track where we are recording. In our earlier example on bouncing, the engineer put the machine into the "sync" mode. This caused the playback head to be turned off completely. The record head became the playback head on all the tracks of music *except* track 23, which is where we were bouncing the combined woodwinds. Since the electrical signals that transfer the sound we hear travel at the speed of light (186,000 miles per second) there is no perceptible delay. This is exactly what happens when we bounce tracks *or* when we overdub a singer, announcer, or instrumentalist. The process is the same whether we use a 24-track machine, a 32-track machine or a 4-track machine.

Go back to the illustration of our track sheet after we did the woodwind bounce. The engineer has decided to put the vocalist for the Crunchies spot on track 17. During the recording process the singer will be listening to the band through a set of earphones (often called "cans") in the studio. Now look at Diagram 4 and notice that all the tracks are shaded gray *except* track 17. The diagram is of the erase and record heads, and the gray tracks indicate where it is acting as a playback head. Notice that track 17, however, is unshaded, since it is acting as a record head. As soon as we are finished recording and want to listen to a playback, the engineer puts the tape recorder in the "normal" mode and everything returns to the way it was: erase head erasing, record head recording, and the playback head playing back. It is *only* in the sync mode that the phenomenon of the record head acting as a playback head occurs.

Remember that the erase head is active in the above example only on track 17. On all other tracks it is disabled while in the sync mode. It will act as an erase head only on the track that is being recorded. What that means is that you are continuously erasing the previous take every time you record a new performance. If you ask your vocalist to sing the Crunchies jingle five times you will be listening to the fifth performance during playback. You will have erased performances one through four. Therefore, if you are in doubt as to whether to save a performance or not, you must start recording onto another available track. Otherwise you will erase the performance and it will be irretrievable at a later time.

Punching

This is another of those terms that sounds more confusing than it really is. Let's assume that while we are recording the Crunchies commercial we find that we don't like the last verse that the vocalist sang. The first verse is fine, however, and we would like to save it. Believe it or not, we can do that! The

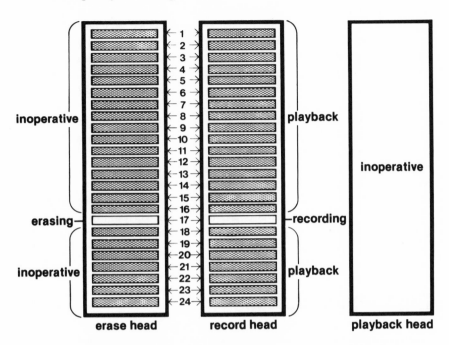

**What the 24-track head assembly looks like in the
sel-synchronization mode. This is how we overdub and bounce.**

Diagram 4

engineer puts the tape recorder in the sync mode (as discussed above) but he
does *not* press the record button. Now the singer is hearing all of the tracks
being played back through her earphones with the record head acting as
playback head on every track *including* track 17. In other words, the singer
is listening to herself sing. At the precise point where we want to replace the
verse the engineer pushes the record button. Instantly the erase head starts
erasing from that point and the record head starts recording on track 17,
exactly as we described the process above.

When we play back the take we will hear the first verse as it *was* and the
new second verse that we just recorded. Today's machines are so good that
you cannot hear the point at which the engineer pushed the record button.

The exciting part is that a good engineer can do more than just punch
in a new verse. He can punch in on mistakes in the band while still keeping
the basic music track intact. As an example, if we recorded a track where
everything was great except for a trumpet mistake, we can punch in that one
trumpet line without having to re-record the entire band or the entire trumpet
part.

There are some precautions to take, however. Once the engineer punches in you will be in the record mode on the track you have chosen. If you decide later that you don't like what you corrected as much as the original, you are out of luck. You will have erased what you already had. If you are not sure that you want to erase the part, try to go onto another track. Otherwise you will have permanently lost what you are trying to correct.

Also, don't try to ask an engineer to make a punch that is just one word or one note. Even a brilliant engineer has human reflexes and the tape recorder cannot be made to do an automatic punch. If the punch point is very tight he may decide that he won't chance it. Remember what we said above: if you make a mistake in the punching process you will have to re-record the material you have lost, since it will have been erased. Use common sense, therefore, in finding punch points. Your engineer not only needs room to punch in, he needs room to **punch out** (stop recording) as well.

Tape Configurations

Ninety-five percent of all radio and TV commercials recorded are mixed down to a **mono** (monaural). This is because TV, AM radio, and many FM stations are not stereo. However, lots of FM radio stations *are* stereo (two channel), and their numbers are growing all the time. We will discuss stereo mixes later, since they are the exception rather than the rule in advertising. Also, the mastery of mono sound is far more important to us, since that is how the bulk of our work will be heard by the public.

The tape copy you get when you leave the studio should be a full-track monaural copy. The very best way to listen to this tape is on a monaural tape deck. Both Sony and Wollensak make top-of-the-line monaural tape decks designed for the advertising industry. (Unfortunately for us, most of the good sound equipment is in stereo since that is the biggest segment of the consumer market.)

A two-track (sometimes called half-track) tape deck (stereo) will play a mono tape. Unfortunately, the two-track tape deck you are likely to have in your office will not be the kind generally found in a professional recording studio, but one designed for the consumer market, which means the playback head will be ¼ track (see diagram 5). As you can see by this illustration, the room allowed for recording and playing back each track is *half* the size of the professional equipment you have been using in the studio and also is not aligned the same way for playback. This means that the stereo deck in your office *will* play a *mono* (full-track) tape but will *not* play a *stereo* tape copy

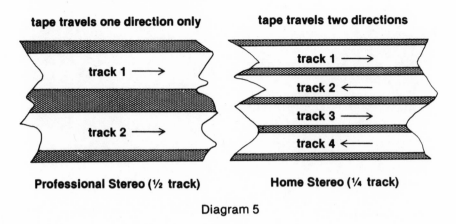

Professional Stereo (½ track)   **Home Stereo (¼ track)**

Diagram 5

that you would normally receive from a recording studio. Simply remember that the best and most useful equipment for an advertising agency is either the mono tape deck or a professional two-track tape recorder.

The Recording Studio

Now comes the moment you have been dreading. You are actually in the studio and wondering how you got there. If this is your first time in a professional recording studio, you are probably feeling as though you wandered onto the set of a Buck Rogers Show. The studio console looks as though it may be used for a rocket launching at any moment, with its thirty-seven faders (the switches that slide up and down and control the recording level of each track), banks of mysterious-looking meters, numerous buttons and gadgets all over the place, plus all of the "outboard" (accessory) gear that may be scattered over the console.

Relax. It isn't necessary for you to know how to rewire the board to have a basic understanding of what it does and how you can use it. During the recording session you will be sitting in the control room, enclosed by glass, with the musicians, singers, and announcers in the *studio* (recording room) on the other side of the glass.

A half hour or so before the scheduled start of your session the engineer and/or assistant engineer will have set up all the microphones and music stands that surround the musicians. The composer-arranger has called in the names of the instruments to be used the day before the session so the studio

A picture of a modern recording studio and console looking out into the studio. The small speakers on the console are for checking your final mix.

personnel could design the way the studio should be setup. If you arrive at the studio and see that everyone is frantically running around setting up music stands and microphones or calibrating the tape recorders, something is wrong. You should be ready to record when your time starts. A 2 PM session should start at 2 PM and not at 2:15. Certainly any delay should not be caused by the studio, and if it is, it should be deducted from your bill. The meter starts when everything is ready to go.

Studios vary greatly in size and design. There are huge, barnlike rooms and small, compact rooms that hold only five or six musicians. Large rooms with high ceilings have quite a bit of natural echo, and this tends to create a live effect on anything recorded in these studios. Generally, big bands sound very good when recorded in a large room. The smaller and more modern studios are often quite "dead," so that the sound on the tape is absolutely electronic without reference to the room itself. This sort of room is great for hard rock. The larger studio operations in New York, Nashville, or Los Angeles usually have more than one recording studio, and the decision about which room to use should be made by your music producer with some input from the studio engineer.

Each microphone in the studio is controlled by a fader on the console. Each fader corresponds to an assigned track on the tape recorder (see diagram 5A). In theory, if all 24 tracks were being used, twenty-four or more faders

A close-up of the console with all
of its knobs, dials and switches.
MCI Corporation.

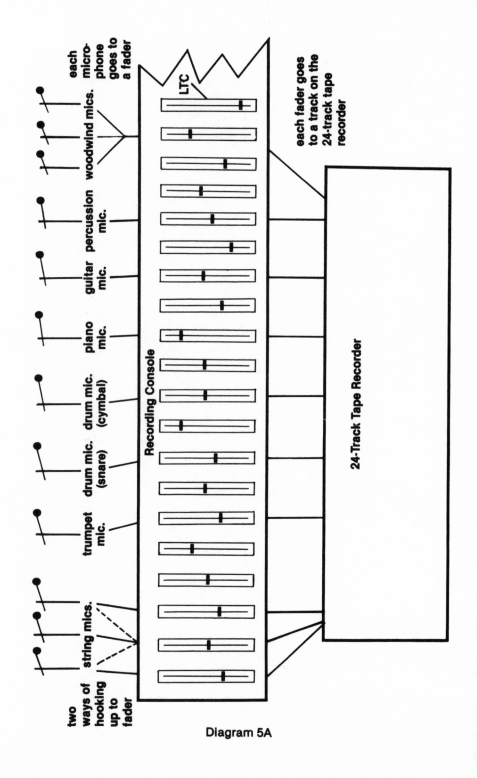

Diagram 5A

would be in use on the console. (More than one fader can go to a given track just as more than one microphone can be assigned to a fader.) The engineer carefully listens to each fader, adjusts the volume level, and then devotes his time to making sure that each instrument sounds good and that the overall sound is clear. During run-throughs with the whole band, he will also check for leakage on critical instruments.

If you are recording a large orchestra there is a good chance that your music producer will decide to record the rhythm section by itself first and then overdub the strings and brass. Usually the overdubs are done right after the rhythm section is sent home. The rhythm section includes the piano, guitars, bass and drums. It may occasionally include some percussion, although this is also frequently added as an overdub.

Many of the buttons and knobs on the console are "equalizers." An equalizer is a very sophisticated tone control that can add or subtract from the various frequency ranges of each instrument. Other buttons on the console control the use of echo. Don't panic. It is not your responsibility to worry about controlling all of this hardware. It is, however, appropriate for you to comment on a particular instrument or sound by saying, for example, "The piano sounds dull. Is there any way for you to make it brighter?" In fact, if this is a session occurring early in your career, ask the engineer to show you what he can do with the equalizers. There is no better way for you to learn. When the engineer hears your comments he will go into action and adjust his knobs and buttons until you and the music producer are satisfied. Don't be surprised if the changes he is making confuse you. You will soon be used to working in a recording studio and find yourself easily able to make distinctions between one sound and another. A typical change might involve simply moving a mike closer to or farther away from a musician. A more serious change can involve changing from one style or brand of microphone to another. Certain mikes have specific purposes. For home use there is an animal called a general-purpose microphone. This is not true in a professional studio. Some mikes record from only one side and some record from any side. Some mikes sound warmer than others. Still other microphones were designed just for drums and other loud instruments. The decision on what microphone to use or not to use is really the engineer's, but you can certainly guide his choice by your preference in the sound you are seeking.

There are two ways to record electric instruments such as the electric guitar and electric piano. The first way is to place a microphone in front of the amplifier that is powering the instrument. It also contains the speaker for the player to hear what he is doing. The second method is called recording "direct." Recording direct bypasses the amplifier. The instrument is "patched" (electronically connected) directly into the recording console itself using a device called a direct box. This eliminates both room and amplifier noises. Since many guitarists rent their amplifiers, or the studio provides them, it is often impossible to get a good clean sound. On the other hand, some players have special amplifiers that produce a unique sound that is hard to match in the studio. Sometimes, if he has enough open tracks, an engineer records an electronic instrument both ways simultaneously on different tracks, creating an interesting blend. Synthesizers are almost always patched directly into the console.

If you have done your homework, you have a pretty good idea of what sound you are after. You've heard a couple of demos and you've told the music house just what it is you are after. For example, a bass is used quite differently in country than it is in disco. It is not a bad idea, if you are after a very specific sound, to bring a copy of a phonograph record that has that sound on it and let your engineer hear it. It is also a big help to the musician to hear something that specific. Don't be afraid of people accusing you of being imitative. Not every audio track forges new ground. Every track can't be full of originality, but it can show new applications for existing sounds.

The Recording Session

During the first part of the recording session the engineer gets a basic sound balance from each individual instrument, making sure that each microphone is working properly. Here is a trick that will mark you as a professional and not an amateur. Don't criticize the sound of an instrument out of context. For example, a bass drum heard alone does not sound interesting or exciting. As the engineer adds the rest of the drum set and then the bass, you will begin to get a feeling of what the music is all about. The recording console is set up so that any instrument can be **soloed** (heard alone). When the engineer presses the solo button all of the other instruments are momentarily muted. Even when you are recording, it is possible to solo an instrument. Even though you will only hear, say, the guitar, all of the instruments are indeed being recorded onto the tape.

Now is a good time for another definition. We will now start using the word **monitor.** For instance, if the overall volume of the music in the control room is satisfactory but you can't hear the guitar, you would ask the engineer to **monitor** the guitar louder. This doesn't mean that the guitar has to be laid down on the tape at a higher level. It simply means that you want to hear what the guitarist is playing at a higher level.

When listening to a playback of a tape, you will be using a section of the console called the monitor system.'' Without a whole lot of explanation, the monitor system enables us to hear a playback of our recording with a rough balance between the instruments. This is essentially the same balance that the musicians hear in their earphones while they are playing. If you don't hear something clearly enough, by all means ask your engineer to monitor something higher or lower.

Different monitor systems vary in sophistication. Some are unable to show you what added equalization would sound like. With other systems, that is no problem. It depends on the recording console the studio has and the way it is designed to be used in the particular studio you are using. As a general rule, monitor systems are *unable* to create all of the nifty sounds you can hear during a mix, so don't waste a lot of time trying to get an engineer to prove to you that a sound is possible to achieve. If he tells you that he can "create it in the final mix," believe him or her. One of the worlds great lies, however, is when an engineer tells you that he can "*fix* it in the mix." If it is on the tape incorrectly, the odds are it will go into the final mix incorrectly.

In general, your communications with the musicians and engineer should be done through the music producer. Your music producer should be able to solve any problems that occur in the session. The studio is a place for executing ideas that were worked out in pre-production meetings. The more discussions that have taken place and understandings that have been reached in advance with the composer, arranger, and producer, the better the recording session should go. A good music producer is quite familiar with the specific talents of each musician and will often write parts utilizing these special abilities. Remember that executing the ideas you have created is as much a talent as coming up with the ideas in the first place. An idea is worthless if the only place it is ever realized is in your mind. Give your producer and engineer a chance to bring your ideas to fruition. Just as your job is creating ideas, their job is executing them.

A number of recording decisions are best left to the engineer. Some of these issues are the use or avoidance of noise reduction devices designed to reduce tape hiss (most studios use either Dolby or DBX), the choice of the brand of recording tape, and the placement of the microphones. If tape hiss is a critical problem on your commercial, your engineer might suggest that you run at 30 ips (*i*nches *p*er *s*econd) or double the normal recording speed. At $250 for a reel of two-inch tape, think twice before you make that decision.

Voiceovers

Many commercials have no music at all but feature the voices of announcers or actors. These dialogue-only commercials are called **voiceover** commercials. (This term was also used earlier to describe a *recording session* where only the announcer(s) are being recorded.) Most actors or announcers who do commercials have audition tapes that contain various commercials or parts of commercials they have already done. By listening carefully to these tapes, also called **demos**, you should be able to find the sound that you want for your commercial. Some adult actors specialize in imitating children's voices, and some can give good imitations of regional or ethnic dialects.

The spoken voice can be affected by the use of echo on the recording console, by the placement and type of microphone used, by use of equalization, or by the various outboard gadgets that are patched into the console. Let an announcer's performance jell a bit before you start to criticize. Criticizing a performer who is just learning copy can make him freeze up and prevent him from taking the creative experimentation that you want.

If you are doing a voiceover for a commercial that has no other sound, i.e. no music or sound effects, you may be able to save considerable money by recording on a monaural machine in a small studio. The studio should have noise reduction, echo, and a reasonably sophisticated console, but you can save a lot of money using ¼-inch tape and by working in a small room. Most of all, make sure that the studio has a competent engineer. Some studios specialize just in voiceovers, and most studios geared to do large music sessions also have a smaller and cheaper room where they do voiceovers.

Flat Recording Vs. Mixed Product

Some engineers prefer to record "flat," that is without adding echo or equalization (using the equalizers we described earlier) to the master tape while it is being recorded. This is true of both music and voiceovers. It allows the engineer and producer the maximum amount of flexibility in the final mix. When you hear a flat tape, however, it will often sound dull, since the only echo or equalization you might hear, if any, is from the monitor section of the console. As we have discussed, this usually allows for only limited effects. Remember, when you hear "Don't worry, we'll fix it in the mix," don't believe it! Make sure that you hear the tape with some kind of echo and equalization. This will give you a good idea of what the final tape will sound like. If the tape still sounds dull, then you know that it can not be fixed in the mix. It is the problem of the music producer to get the mix you want as well as the mix you need. It is your job to decide what you like and what is not acceptable.

Singers

Singers use the same type of demo reels that announcers do. The music producer selects session musicians, often with the help of a music contractor, who is usually a playing musician who calls and books the rest of the band. Singers are usually selected by agreement between the music house and the agency. If the agency and the composer disagree about which singer is best for a spot, and if the budget permits it, it is always possible to record two singers against the same instrumental track. Both singers must be paid for the session and then the choice can be made as to which singer sounds better. With a 24-track machine and two open tracks, recording a second singer is a very simple matter. Since the band has long since gone, the expense of recording the singers is minimal. The real money for singers is not in the session fees but in the **residuals.** Residuals are the reuse fees that the singers get when the commercial is run on air. The session fees themselves are relatively low. Only the singer who is used gets the reuse fees from the commercials, so recording two or more singers does not obligate you to any residuals except to that singer who is actually used on the commercial.

Multiple Tracking—The Overdub Sound

Many of the commercials on the air today sound as though twenty-five or thirty people were hired to do the singing. In fact, there are often no more than four or five singers who have each been recorded four or more times. This is called "multiple tracking" or "multing" (sounds like a phrase the Audubon Society might use.) The reason for "multing" is that it is considerably less expensive than hiring twenty or thirty singers. The governing unions, The Screen Actors Guild (SAG) and The American Federation of Television and Radio Artists (AFTRA), only charge 50% above the session scale for a singer to multiple track. These singers are fast, excellent sight readers and improvisers, and they can adjust their performance style to go with your music track. By using four or five top professionals who are acccustomed to working together you can get exactly the right sound and get it fast. Don't waste money by trying to save money. Professional singers are a perfect example of the fact that using the right talent the first time can indeed save you money. Dick Weissman once had to do a Beach Boys-style vocal for a film score that he was recording in Denver. Dick spent more than ten hours in the studio trying to get the right sound and never succeeded. He traveled to New York and got it in one hour flat. And this is not an isolated story.

Because the residuals paid singers are so high, particularly on a major product that is scheduled to run on network television, certain singers make a practice of putting the music producer on hold until the last minute. The singer figures that if a more lucrative session comes up he or she can cancel your session. The chances are that a major account will not be willing to reschedule their session to accommodate singers. If your own session isn't as critical and doesn't really require a very specific vocal sound then be reasonable and let them out of your commercial so that they can do their network spot. As we've said before, courtesy *does* count and singers, musicians, and composers alike earn their living through advertising.

When you go into the studio you should have a clear idea of what you want from the singers. Nothing is worse than spending two hours hassling with a vocal part and ending up with exactly what you heard two hours ago. You need to develop a feel for when a performance is perfect, when it is acceptable, and when it doesn't work. As we have already discussed in the sections on voiceovers, let the singer work up an interpretation of a part before you get too critical. Although it is best that you not talk to the musicians, it is a good idea to work closely with the singers. Ask their advice, encourage them, and make sure that the lyrics are clear, and that the essential points of your Crunchies spot can be understood by a two-year-old Eskimo. Once the singers have left the studio the product is ready for all of the finishing touches: the mix session.

The Final Mix

The mix is truly the most exciting part of the recording process. It is the time when all of the elements that we have recorded on the 24-track will be balanced, echoed, equalized, and adjusted. It is the first time that we will hear everything as it will be in its final form. It is a very creative process, as you will see. The engineer, possibly an assistant engineer, the music producer, and you representing the agency, are usually the only people present at a final mix. And the fewer the better, since this is a time for careful listening.

You will now move from the monitor system that we described earlier to the full console. All of the myriad possibilities that the console and its inboard and outboard equipment can supply are yours for the asking. Now all your energies can be concentrated on listening and enhancing the material already recorded. We will be mixing our twenty-four track tape of the Crunchies commercial down to a monaural, full-track tape for use on AM radio. If we were mixing a TV commercial, the final mixed tape would have to be inserted into the film or videotape, as we will describe in part two of this book.

The engineer will again listen to each track individually, making sure each instrument sounds just the way it should. The producer helps by giving the engineer his input as well. If some musical mistakes are uncovered several options are available. If the mistake is trivial, leaving it alone or "dipping" (lowering) the fader slightly during the mix will probably be sufficient. The mistake simply blends into the music track. If the mistake is significant, it may be necessary to **key out** (delete) the offending section. Obviously, you can't key out a trumpet mistake in the middle of a solo and not have it noticed. there will be those times when, unless you are willing to go to the expense of recalling the particular musican and re-recording his or her part, all you can do is grin and bear it. Thankfully, this is not something that happens very often. If you pay attention during the recording session and try to limit outside distractions (like phone calls) during the time that the track is being recorded, the above examples will almost never be a problem. After all, with you, the music producer, and composer, and the engineer all listening at the same time, one of you should catch the mistake.

Assuming no mistakes have turned up, the engineer will set the volume levels, noting the proper volume of each track. Now is really not the time to be on the phone. It is especially distracting if the phone is nearby and pulls you away from the mix at a time when your concentration should not be broken.

Once the volume levels are set the real work begins. Equalization and echo can be added to all or some of the tracks to enhance the sound. At this point everyone's full attention is necessary.

We should remind you that if you are dissatisfied with the sound of an instrument or voice, be sure to tell the engineer and producer what is bothering you. A reasonable comment is "The trumpets sound very tinny. Can't you make them sound richer?" Simply saying that the trumpets sound bad is of no real help. The better you can learn to express what you are thinking, the faster and more efficiently an engineer can fulfill your wishes.

Also remember that you could stay in the studio for hours and hours doing a mix. The chances are, though, that your budget doesn't allow for that. A lot of the production that you hear on your favorite record is not attainable without spending a lot of time in the mix. It is unfair to ask your producer to get "that Bee Gee's vocal sound" in a one-hour mix. It just won't happen. If it is that important to you, budget the time for it. Budgets that are saleable by the agency to the client require some give and take in the final product. If you want to sound like Coke or McDonald's or the Bee Gee's, be prepared to spend the time and therefore the money. If not, understand that there are trade-offs that you will have to make in the studio. This is a *very* important point and one that is far too often overlooked when planning a session.

Back to the mix. The adjustment of volume levels and decisions on the use of echo and equalization may take the engineer and producer thirty minutes or more for the average spot, so don't be impatient. This is truly a time, as we said above, where you get what you pay for.

At the end of this process you should be ready to take a pass (attempt) at a mix. This requires running the 24-track and monaural machines simultaneously. The mono machine will be *recording* the mix you are creating in its final usable form: a ¼-inch mono tape (see diagram 6).

After you have completed the first mix, listen to it, making sure that all of the important elements on the 24-track tape are present in the relative balances that you want to hear. It is critical that the announcer or singer be clearly audible over the instrumental background. There is a basic difference between mixing commercials and mixing records. Many rock records are mixed in such a way that the lyrics are not clearly audible. Because of that fact, the artists often print the lyrics of a new song somewhere on the jacket or inner sleeve of the record. A mix of this kind in a commercial would probably be suicide. Your client is paying to have the product name and all key selling points clearly audible to the listener.

The only thing that records and advertising have in common is the language of music. The application of that language in the two different media of advertising and phonograph records is as different as night and day.

When you listen to the mix be sure to try it on a small speaker, the type of speaker in a small radio or television set. (Most studios that do a lot of work in advertising have a speaker like this in the control room.) This is the way it will sound to the average consumer. The $1000 speakers in the studio are marvelous, but they don't give you an accurate idea of what the consumer will hear in his living room.

Also, be careful not to listen at a volume level that is too high. This is also unrealistic. A highly rhythmic music track should sound just as good played softly as it does played loudly.

You will probably need to try at least four or five mixes of your spot before you are completely satisfied. Once you start the actual mixing, as opposed to just setting the volume levels, you should have your finished mix within twenty minutes. The four or five different mixes will reflect the feelings of your engineer, the music producer, and the guidance that you have to offer them. Since ¼-inch tape, the type used for monaural mixing, is relatively cheap, it is standard practice to keep all of your mixes for comparison. Sometimes you like the opening of one mix and the closing of another. It is very common to splice the two parts together to create the final mix.

No two mixes will sound identical. If you are unsure which mix came out best, or if you are unsure how your boss or client will react to a mix, take copies of the two best mixes back to the agency for study before you make a decision as to which one will be your final choice.

The way that you will mix a voiceover depends largely what the com-

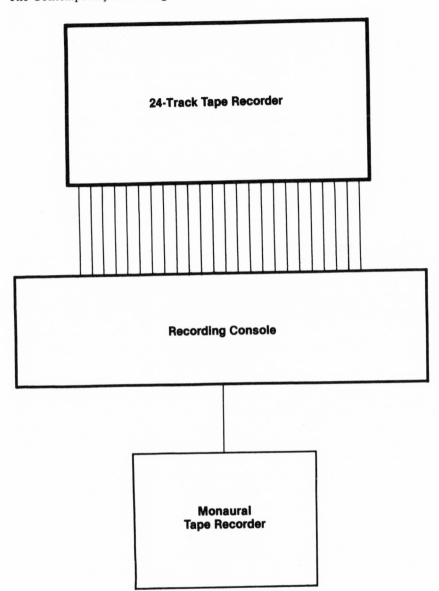

24-track mixdown to monaural

Diagram 6

mercial is selling and why. A one-week grocery special will probably be mixed rather loudly, particularly that part announcing the special. If you are mixing an institutional spot for a company like IBM you will want a more distinguished, softer approach in keeping with the corporate image. Don't forget the relationship of your spot to the age group you are trying to reach. If you are doing a heavy rock spot for a top-40 format radio station, the spot should sound like the music of the station, i.e. loud and confident. If your spot is aimed at a classical-music radio station, a heavy-rock sound will probably annoy the listeners and sound ridiculous on that station. The engineer and music producer are well aware of these demographic distinctions, and if you can clearly explain what you are trying to do, they will help you to make the right decisions.

Stereo Mixes

A mix intended for an FM radio station should be a stereo or two-track mix. In this case you will mix down from 24 tracks to *two*. You now have the choice of putting instruments and voices on the left, right, center, or inbetween. If you really want to be surprised, wait until you see all of the possibilities of placement there are in a mix. Ask your engineer to **pan** a track from full right to full left at your next session and you'll get an idea of what we mean.

This stereo separation takes more pre-production and more experience with the equipment than a mono mix. Most music producers avoid stereo mixes unless they know that they will be running on an FM stereo station.

As video tape recorders and video disks become more commonplace in the American home there will undoubtedly be more emphasis on sound with video, and surely stereo sound in full fidelity will finally be an everyday affair. At the writing of this book, a major cable packager, Warner-Amex, announced a 24-hour video music channel called MTV (Music Television) for cable television, where the audio portion would be simulcast in stereo over a local FM radio station. If this is the future of entertainment, then it will probably be the future of advertising as well. We have noticed a sharp increase in the use of stereo mixes in advertising. As the technology changes, so does the industry.

Different Versions of the Same Commercial

Many long-running campaigns are based on one specific :30 or :60 spot. The complete original version is a full lyric version, which announces a campaign.

The next version is called a "donut." Usually the commercial opens with a line or two of the full lyric version and then goes to just the instrumental (no singers) and closes with a sung tag or **billboard,** as it is sometimes called. The last evolution is a commercial opening with an instrumental and continuing all the way to the end and closing with a billboard. Obviously, these formats are not etched in stone, but are commonly used in today's advertising.

If the original version is intelligently planned and pre-produced, a re-mix is all that may be necessary to create room for the announcer copy. A smaller client would be particularly happy at the savings realized in not having to go back into the studio for a whole new session. Even a larger client tries to save money where possible.

If you are creating a piece of music that you expect to last more than one "cycle" (thirteen weeks) then careful consideration of the factors discussed above is another element that you should remember in your pre-production meetings.

Where to Record

If you are doing a national spot, the chances are that you will want to record it in New York. Studios, musicians, and singers in New York are accustomed to recording commercials, and they are set up to handle the work quickly and efficiently. There may be instances when you may not want to record in New York. If you are doing a commercial aimed at, say, professional truck drivers, and have decided that a C&W (Country & Western) music track is the correct marketing approach, you may want to record in Nashville, the home of country-music. Nashville has a unique talent pool of country-music singers and musicians. Some of these sounds cannot be matched in New York, although they can be imitated. If you go to Nashville to record, be sure that the studio you are using has all of the equipment that you need. Your music producer should be familiar with out-of-town studios in major production centers.

If you are not sure of the musical direction of your spot, you are probably better off staying in New York, particularly if you are seeking more of a pop or rock sound.

Other reasons to record in different cities may involve the product headquarters of your client, or the talent used on the commercial. It may be cheaper to fly you and a music producer to record a seven-piece rock band in Chicago than to bring them all to New York. If you go elsewhere to record a commercial, make clear that you expect to pay union scales, since your agency is surely a signatory to all of the major union agreements. Although **scales** (minimum salaries) for commercials are set nationally, there is a certain amount of local or regional autonomy allowed by the national unions. In some instances local or regional spots can be done cheaper in the home market, with approval of the unions. In no instance should you have to pay above scale. The sole exeption to this is if you use a celebrity for endorsement value. In that case you will probably be negotiating yearly minimums and guarantees. This is best left to the business affairs department and not to the producer or writer. Nothing is worse than finding yourself married to a bad deal where a spokesperson is getting paid a king's ransom, and has become a very integral part of the campaign.

If this celebrity is to remain as an on- or off-camera spokesperson for any great length of time, you can count on the price of that endorsement getting higher as time goes by, not lower. The reasoning is that if the spokesperson is proving so successful that you want to renew the contract, it must be worth more to the advertiser.

There are a number of commercials that are recorded in markets like Denver or Omaha that are done nonunion. Studios are cheaper in these towns and sometimes the musicians are willing to work for less than union scale. This could end up costing you money in the long run because many of the recording studios outside major markets don't have backup equipment or state-of-the-art recording consoles. If your commercial goes regional instead of local or national instead of regional, you can encounter considerable trouble with the performing unions involved, and a union could take away the agency's franchise to produce. This could be more than just costly to your agency because it would essentially prevent you from producing national spots. Although there are good musicians and singers in most major towns, there isn't the depth of talent or technical equipment that you find in the major recording centers.

Summary of Roles in the Studio

Now that we have explained the recording process, let's go back and summarize what each person's responsibilites are in the recording process.

The engineer is in charge of all the technical aspects of the recording. This includes the selection and set-up of the mikes, selection of noise reduction equipment (if any) and the type of tape to be used on the session, plus the actual handling of the equipment.

The music producer chooses the musicians or hires a contractor to do so. The composer-arranger writes and arranges the music, or jobs the arrangement to someone else. The composer and arranger are usually in the studio itself while the musicians are recording. Most arrangers use a music copyist to copy all of the individual music parts from an orchestral master score that the composer has prepared. It is not unusual for mistakes to crop up in the copying process, but they are usually obvious and quickly corrected by the composer or arranger with the aid of the musicians.

The agency producer is the overall supervisor of the product, making sure that all of the parts are coming together as planned, checking to see that the lyrics are correct and easily understood, and that all timings are correct and workable. The agency producer should not hesitate to ask questions at each step of the process taking care not to create a feeling of harassment. Be sure that singers, announcers, and musicians have had sufficent time to develop some sort of performance from your original directions before you start to criticize their work.

None of the people in the studio can function to maximum effectiveness unless everyone works together as a team. Everyone in the studio wants to make the best possible commercial. If the agency producer keeps this goal in mind, and if the music production team has been selected with proper care, working in the studio should be an enjoyable and profitable experience for all involved.

Remember, the studio is the place where all of the elements that the copywriter, art director, agency producer, and composer shared only in concept finally come to life. With sound pre-production (no pun intended) the work you do in the studio should be fun as well as effective. The finished execution should be a tribute to your efforts, and the lack of problems an example of your professionalism.

PART TWO

How Sound and Picture Work Together

Film Mathematics

The integration of sound with film is a process that involves the use of some simple mathematics. More importantly it requires an understanding of the basic difference between the way a tape machine operates and the way a movie projector works. But first, here is a very important point that should be committed to memory: With the exception of 8-millimeter (mm) film, which is used for nonprofessional purposes, all *professional* film, whether it is 16mm or 35mm, operates at twenty-four frames *per second*. This is true of Cinemascope and Panavision, too. The word millimeter (mm) refers to the actual size of a single frame of film.

Here are two other facts that must be committed to memory: 35mm film has sixteen frames *per foot* of film, while 16mm film has forty frames *per foot*.

The mathematics of using sound with film can be fairly complex. Carrol Knudsen and Mark Fredricks have written books detailing the relationship between feet of film and minutes and seconds of time. They also have worked out tables that will tell you the length of music in minutes and seconds if a beat of music is adjusted to a specific speed. This is usually expressed in the form of a metronome setting and, as we shall see shortly, in terms of a click track. Conversion charts, referred to as "Ready Eddies," can be purchased at professional film supply houses. These simple conversion charts express feet of film in terms of minutes and seconds of time.

The specifics of film mathematics are best left to your music production house, but Earle Hagen, in his book *Scoring for Films,* points out that in the 35mm configuration the ratio of film to time is three feet of film for every two seconds of time. This ratio expressed numerically is 3/2. This means that a thirty-second commercial in 35mm would use forty-five feet of film. If you don't believe this, work it out. Remember those two facts that you committed to memory: 35mm film has sixteen frames per foot and runs at twenty-four frames per second, or a foot-and-a-half of film for every second of time.

None of the above math is necessary for you in your day-to-day duties if you are a copywriter, art director, or agency producer. It is important, however, for you to have a basic understanding of film so that you can work comfortably and competently with your suppliers.

Click Track

Some composers have an extraordinary knack of being able to work accurately with a specific number of seconds or minutes of film. To avoid time snarls in the studio most composers prefer to work with an electronic device called a "click track." A click track is similar to a metronome in that it sets a specific tempo. But other than that, the two systems are quite different. A metronome measures tempo in beats of music *per minute*. Therefore a metronome setting of 120 translates to 120 beats per minutes, or ½ second for every beat of music. This is fine for the piano student trying to practice his Mozart, but it is of no help in dealing with film.

We want to know our tempo in relation to film. Remember that film runs at twenty-four frames per second. It always remains at a *constant* speed. Musical tempos, however, *vary* from one musical piece to the next. Some go fast and some go slowly. Therefore, a click track was designed to measure how many frames of film have passed through the projector for *each beat* of music. With this system, an arranger or composer can accurately start figuring his visual cues into his musical composition. A moderate tempo would be a 12-0 click. The "12" means that each beat of music takes an even twelve frames of film, or ½ second. (Remember, film runs at twenty-four frames a second.) A 7-0 click means that each beat of music is equal to exactly seven frames of film.

The second number of the click track (the "0" in the examples above) refers to eighths of a frame of film. There are, in 35mm, four sprocket holes per frame. It was decided that if tempos for click were measured in increments of ½ sprocket holes, the accuracy would be more than sufficient. Therefore, a 12-7 click means that 12⅞ frames of film is equal to one beat of music. There could be no 12-8 click, since that would mean 12⅝ frames of film per beat of music. Instead, it would be expressed as a 13-0 click.

If you look at diagram 7 you will see what a typical page of a click-track book looks like. Tempos run from a 6-0 click, which is quite fast, to a 36-0 click, which is quite slow.

It is useful to know that the higher the number of the click, the slower the tempo. Conversely, the lower the number of the click, the faster the tempo. A 17-0 (17⅞'s) click is very slow. A 7-1 (7⅛) click is very fast.

Click can also be measured in terms of time for use with videotape or radio. See diagram 8 for a sample page of this method of measuring tempo.

The conductor of your jingle can make sure that all of the cues in your film are precisely reflected in the music by utilizing click track. For example, a cymbal crash comes out exactly as the pie gets thrown in the face of the hero, rather than a second earlier or later.

Composers utilize click track in different ways. Some composers prefer

THE TEMPO IS 11.750 FRAMES PER BEAT (11-6) — METRONOME – 122.56 — PAGE NO.47

click #	0	1	2	3	4	5	6	7	8	9
0	0 - 0	0 -12	1 - 8	2 - 3	2 -15	3 -11	4 - 7	5 - 2	5 -14	6 -10
10	7 - 6	8 - 1	8 -13	9 - 9	10 - 5	11 - 0	11 -12	12 - 8	13 - 4	13 -15
20	14 -11	15 - 7	16 - 3	16 -14	17 -10	18 - 6	19 - 2	19 -13	20 - 9	21 - 5
30	22 - 1	22 -12	23 - 8	24 - 4	25 - 0	25 -11	26 - 7	27 - 3	27 -15	28 -10
40	29 - 6	30 - 2	30 -14	31 - 9	32 - 5	33 - 1	33 -13	34 - 8	35 - 4	36 - 0
50	36 -12	37 - 7	38 - 3	38 -15	39 -11	40 - 6	41 - 2	41 -14	42 -10	43 - 5
60	44 - 1	44 -13	45 - 9	46 - 4	47 - 0	47 -12	48 - 8	49 - 3	49 -15	50 -11
70	51 - 7	52 - 2	52 -14	53 -10	54 - 6	55 - 1	55 -13	56 - 9	57 - 5	58 - 0
80	58 -12	59 - 8	60 - 4	60 -15	61 -11	62 - 7	63 - 3	63 -14	64 -10	65 - 6
90	66 - 2	66 -13	67 - 9	68 - 5	69 - 1	69 -12	70 - 8	71 - 4	72 - 0	72 -11
100	73 - 7	74 - 3	74 -15	75 -10	76 - 6	77 - 2	77 -14	78 - 9	79 - 5	80 - 1
110	80 -13	81 - 8	82 - 4	83 - 0	83 -12	84 - 7	85 - 3	85 -15	86 -11	87 - 6
120	88 - 2	88 -14	89 -10	90 - 5	91 - 1	91 -13	92 - 9	93 - 4	94 - 0	94 -12
130	95 - 8	96 - 3	96 -15	97 -11	98 - 7	99 - 2	99 -14	100 -10	101 - 6	102 - 1
140	102 -13	103 - 9	104 - 5	105 - 0	105 -12	106 - 8	107 - 4	107 -15	108 -11	109 - 7
150	110 - 3	110 -14	111 -10	112 - 6	113 - 2	113 -13	114 - 9	115 - 5	116 - 1	116 -12
160	117 - 8	118 - 4	119 - 0	119 -11	120 - 7	121 - 3	121 -15	122 -10	123 - 6	124 - 2
170	124 -14	125 - 9	126 - 5	127 - 1	127 -13	128 - 8	129 - 4	130 - 0	130 -12	131 - 7
180	132 - 3	132 -15	133 -11	134 - 6	135 - 2	135 -14	136 -10	137 - 5	138 - 1	138 -13
190	139 - 9	140 - 4	141 - 0	141 -12	142 - 8	143 - 3	143 -15	144 -11	145 - 7	146 - 2
200	146 -14	147 -10	148 - 6	149 - 1	149 -13	150 - 9	151 - 5	152 - 0	152 -12	153 - 8
210	154 - 4	154 -15	155 -11	156 - 7	157 - 3	157 -14	158 -10	159 - 6	160 - 2	160 -13
220	161 - 9	162 - 5	163 - 1	163 -12	164 - 8	165 - 4	166 - 0	166 -11	167 - 7	168 - 3
230	168 -15	169 -10	170 - 6	171 - 2	171 -14	172 - 9	173 - 5	174 - 1	174 -13	175 - 8
240	176 - 4	177 - 0	177 -12	178 - 7	179 - 3	179 -15	180 -11	181 - 6	182 - 2	182 -14
250	183 -10	184 - 5	185 - 1	185 -13	186 - 9	187 - 4	188 - 0	188 -12	189 - 8	190 - 3
260	190 -15	191 -11	192 - 7	193 - 2	193 -14	194 -10	195 - 6	196 - 1	196 -13	197 - 9
270	198 - 5	199 - 0	199 -12	200 - 8	201 - 4	201 -15	202 -11	203 - 7	204 - 3	204 -14
280	205 -10	206 - 6	207 - 2	207 -13	208 - 9	209 - 5	210 - 1	210 -12	211 - 8	212 - 4
290	213 - 0	213 -11	214 - 7	215 - 3	215 -15	216 -10	217 - 6	218 - 2	218 -14	219 - 9
300	220 - 5	221 - 1	221 -13	222 - 8	223 - 4	224 - 0	224 -12	225 - 7	226 - 3	226 -15
310	227 -11	228 - 6	229 - 2	229 -14	230 -10	231 - 5	232 - 1	232 -13	233 - 9	234 - 4
320	235 - 0	235 -12	236 - 8	237 - 3	237 -15	238 -11	239 - 7	240 - 2	240 -14	241 -10
330	242 - 6	243 - 1	243 -13	244 - 9	245 - 5	246 - 0	246 -12	247 - 8	248 - 4	248 -15
340	249 -11	250 - 7	251 - 3	251 -14	252 -10	253 - 6	254 - 2	254 -13	255 - 9	256 - 5
350	257 - 1	257 -12	258 - 8	259 - 4	260 - 0	260 -11	261 - 7	262 - 3	262 -15	263 -10
360	264 - 6	265 - 2	265 -14	266 - 9	267 - 5	268 - 1	268 -13	269 - 8	270 - 4	271 - 0
370	271 -12	272 - 7	273 - 3	273 -15	274 -11	275 - 6	276 - 2	276 -14	277 -10	278 - 5
380	279 - 1	279 -13	280 - 9	281 - 4	282 - 0	282 -12	283 - 8	284 - 3	284 -15	285 -11
390	286 - 7	287 - 2	287 -14	288 -10	289 - 6	290 - 1	290 -13	291 - 9	292 - 5	293 - 0
400	293 -12	294 - 8	295 - 4	295 -15	296 -11	297 - 7	298 - 3	298 -14	299 -10	300 - 6
410	301 - 2	301 -13	302 - 9	303 - 5	304 - 1	304 -12	305 - 8	306 - 4	307 - 0	307 -11
420	308 - 7	309 - 3	309 -15	310 -10	311 - 6	312 - 2	312 -14	313 - 9	314 - 5	315 - 1
430	315 -13	316 - 8	317 - 4	318 - 0	318 -12	319 - 7	320 - 3	320 -15	321 -11	322 - 6
440	323 - 2	323 -14	324 -10	325 - 5	326 - 1	326 -13	327 - 9	328 - 4	329 - 0	329 -12
450	330 - 8	331 - 3	331 -15	332 -11	333 - 7	334 - 2	334 -14	335 -10	336 - 6	337 - 1
460	337 -13	338 - 9	339 - 5	340 - 0	340 -12	341 - 8	342 - 4	342 -15	343 -11	344 - 7
470	345 - 3	345 -14	346 -10	347 - 6	348 - 2	348 -13	349 - 9	350 - 5	351 - 1	351 -12
480	352 - 8	353 - 4	354 - 0	354 -11	355 - 7	356 - 3	356 -15	357 -10	358 - 6	359 - 2
490	359 -14	360 - 9	361 - 5	362 - 1	362 -13	363 - 8	364 - 4	365 - 0	365 -12	366 - 7
500	367 - 3	367 -15	368 -11	369 - 6	370 - 2	370 -14	371 -10	372 - 5	373 - 1	373 -13
510	374 - 9	375 - 4	376 - 0	376 -12	377 - 8	378 - 3	378 -15	379 -11	380 - 7	381 - 2
520	381 -14	382 -10	383 - 6	384 - 1	384 -13	385 - 9	386 - 5	387 - 0	387 -12	388 - 8
530	389 - 4	389 -15	390 -11	391 - 7	392 - 3	392 -14	393 -10	394 - 6	395 - 2	395 -13
540	396 - 9	397 - 5	398 - 1	398 -12	399 - 8	400 - 4	401 - 0	401 -11	402 - 7	403 - 3
550	403 -15	404 -10	405 - 6	406 - 2	406 -14	407 - 9	408 - 5	409 - 1	409 -13	410 - 8
560	411 - 4	412 - 0	412 -12	413 - 7	414 - 3	414 -15	415 -11	416 - 6	417 - 2	417 -14
570	418 -10	419 - 5	420 - 1	420 -13	421 - 9	422 - 4	423 - 0	423 -12	424 - 8	425 - 3
580	425 -15	426 -11	427 - 7	428 - 2	428 -14	429 -10	430 - 6	431 - 1	431 -13	432 - 9
590	433 - 5	434 - 0	434 -12	435 - 8	436 - 4	436 -15	437 -11	438 - 7	439 - 3	439 -14

A typical page from Project Tempo, a click-track book often used by arrangers working with film. This page is for 35 mm film.

Diagram 7

that all of the musicians hear the click track in their headphones so that all of the tempos come out exactly right. Others feed the click only to the rhythm section figuring once the rhythm is accurately captured on tape the other musicians can play along with the rhythm track. A few composers, such as the famous film composer Erich Wolfgang Korngold, do not use the click track at all. Such a composer feels that a metronome doesn't "swing." In other words, mechanical accuracy should be the problem of the conductor. The idea is to give the musicians some room to interpret the music while the conductor makes sure that the rhythm remains accurate.

This is not the place for an extended theoretical discussion on the aesthetics of click track vs. the problems of achieving correct tempos without the click track. We have raised the issue to make sure that you are aware that

THE TEMPO IS 11.750 FRAMES PER BEAT (11-6) METRONOME - 122.56 PAGE NO. 47

click #	0	1	2	3	4	5	6	7	8	9
0	.00	.00	.49	.98	1.47	1.96	2.45	2.94	3.43	3.92
10	4.41	4.90	5.39	5.88	6.37	6.86	7.35	7.84	8.33	8.82
20	9.31	9.80	10.29	10.78	11.27	11.75	12.24	12.73	13.22	13.71
30	14.20	14.69	15.18	15.67	16.16	16.65	17.14	17.63	18.12	18.61
40	19.10	19.59	20.08	20.57	21.06	21.55	22.04	22.53	23.02	23.50
50	23.99	24.48	24.97	25.46	25.95	26.44	26.93	27.42	27.91	28.40
60	28.89	29.38	29.87	30.36	30.85	31.34	31.83	32.32	32.81	33.30
70	33.79	34.28	34.77	35.25	35.74	36.23	36.72	37.21	37.70	38.19
80	38.68	39.17	39.66	40.15	40.64	41.13	41.62	42.11	42.60	43.09
90	43.58	44.07	44.56	45.05	45.54	46.03	46.52	47.00	47.49	47.98
100	48.47	48.96	49.45	49.94	50.43	50.92	51.41	51.90	52.39	52.88
110	53.37	53.86	54.35	54.84	55.33	55.82	56.31	56.80	57.29	57.78
120	0/ 58.27	0/ 58.75	0/ 59.24	0/ 59.73	1/ .22	1/ .71	1/ 1.20	1/ 1.69	1/ 2.18	1/ 2.67
130	1/ 3.16	1/ 3.65	1/ 4.14	1/ 4.63	1/ 5.12	1/ 5.61	1/ 6.10	1/ 6.59	1/ 7.08	1/ 7.57
140	1/ 8.06	1/ 8.55	1/ 9.04	1/ 9.53	1/ 10.02	1/ 10.50	1/ 10.99	1/ 11.48	1/ 11.97	1/ 12.46
150	1/ 12.95	1/ 13.44	1/ 13.93	1/ 14.42	1/ 14.91	1/ 15.40	1/ 15.89	1/ 16.38	1/ 16.87	1/ 17.36
160	1/ 17.85	1/ 18.34	1/ 18.83	1/ 19.32	1/ 19.81	1/ 20.30	1/ 20.79	1/ 21.28	1/ 21.77	1/ 22.25
170	1/ 22.74	1/ 23.23	1/ 23.72	1/ 24.21	1/ 24.70	1/ 25.19	1/ 25.68	1/ 26.17	1/ 26.66	1/ 27.15
180	1/ 27.64	1/ 28.13	1/ 28.62	1/ 29.11	1/ 29.60	1/ 30.09	1/ 30.58	1/ 31.07	1/ 31.56	1/ 32.05
190	1/ 32.54	1/ 33.03	1/ 33.52	1/ 34.00	1/ 34.49	1/ 34.98	1/ 35.47	1/ 35.96	1/ 36.45	1/ 36.94
200	1/ 37.43	1/ 37.92	1/ 38.41	1/ 38.90	1/ 39.39	1/ 39.88	1/ 40.37	1/ 40.86	1/ 41.35	1/ 41.84
210	1/ 42.33	1/ 42.82	1/ 43.31	1/ 43.80	1/ 44.29	1/ 44.78	1/ 45.27	1/ 45.75	1/ 46.24	1/ 46.73
220	1/ 47.22	1/ 47.71	1/ 48.20	1/ 48.69	1/ 49.18	1/ 49.67	1/ 50.16	1/ 50.65	1/ 51.14	1/ 51.63
230	1/ 52.12	1/ 52.61	1/ 53.10	1/ 53.59	1/ 54.08	1/ 54.57	1/ 55.06	1/ 55.55	1/ 56.04	1/ 56.53
240	1/ 57.02	1/ 57.50	1/ 57.99	1/ 58.48	1/ 58.97	1/ 59.46	1/ 59.95	2/ .44	2/ .93	2/ 1.42
250	2/ 1.91	2/ 2.40	2/ 2.89	2/ 3.38	2/ 3.87	2/ 4.36	2/ 4.85	2/ 5.34	2/ 5.83	2/ 6.32
260	2/ 6.81	2/ 7.30	2/ 7.79	2/ 8.28	2/ 8.77	2/ 9.25	2/ 9.74	2/ 10.23	2/ 10.72	2/ 11.21
270	2/ 11.70	2/ 12.19	2/ 12.68	2/ 13.17	2/ 13.66	2/ 14.15	2/ 14.64	2/ 15.13	2/ 15.62	2/ 16.11
280	2/ 16.60	2/ 17.09	2/ 17.58	2/ 18.07	2/ 18.56	2/ 19.05	2/ 19.54	2/ 20.03	2/ 20.52	2/ 21.00
290	2/ 21.49	2/ 21.98	2/ 22.47	2/ 22.96	2/ 23.45	2/ 23.94	2/ 24.43	2/ 24.92	2/ 25.41	2/ 25.90
300	2/ 26.39	2/ 26.88	2/ 27.37	2/ 27.86	2/ 28.35	2/ 28.84	2/ 29.33	2/ 29.82	2/ 30.31	2/ 30.80
310	2/ 31.29	2/ 31.78	2/ 32.27	2/ 32.75	2/ 33.24	2/ 33.73	2/ 34.22	2/ 34.71	2/ 35.20	2/ 35.69
320	2/ 36.18	2/ 36.67	2/ 37.16	2/ 37.65	2/ 38.14	2/ 38.63	2/ 39.12	2/ 39.61	2/ 40.10	2/ 40.59
330	2/ 41.08	2/ 41.57	2/ 42.06	2/ 42.55	2/ 43.04	2/ 43.53	2/ 44.02	2/ 44.50	2/ 44.99	2/ 45.48
340	2/ 45.97	2/ 46.46	2/ 46.95	2/ 47.44	2/ 47.93	2/ 48.42	2/ 48.91	2/ 49.40	2/ 49.89	2/ 50.38
350	2/ 50.87	2/ 51.36	2/ 51.85	2/ 52.34	2/ 52.83	2/ 53.32	2/ 53.81	2/ 54.30	2/ 54.79	2/ 55.28
360	2/ 55.77	2/ 56.25	2/ 56.74	2/ 57.23	2/ 57.72	2/ 58.21	2/ 58.70	2/ 59.19	2/ 59.68	3/ .17
370	3/ .66	3/ 1.15	3/ 1.64	3/ 2.13	3/ 2.62	3/ 3.11	3/ 3.60	3/ 4.09	3/ 4.58	3/ 5.07
380	3/ 5.56	3/ 6.05	3/ 6.54	3/ 7.03	3/ 7.52	3/ 8.00	3/ 8.49	3/ 8.98	3/ 9.47	3/ 9.96
390	3/ 10.45	3/ 10.94	3/ 11.43	3/ 11.92	3/ 12.41	3/ 12.90	3/ 13.39	3/ 13.88	3/ 14.37	3/ 14.86
400	3/ 15.35	3/ 15.84	3/ 16.33	3/ 16.82	3/ 17.31	3/ 17.80	3/ 18.29	3/ 18.78	3/ 19.27	3/ 19.75
410	3/ 20.24	3/ 20.73	3/ 21.22	3/ 21.71	3/ 22.20	3/ 22.69	3/ 23.18	3/ 23.67	3/ 24.16	3/ 24.65
420	3/ 25.14	3/ 25.63	3/ 26.12	3/ 26.61	3/ 27.10	3/ 27.59	3/ 28.08	3/ 28.57	3/ 29.06	3/ 29.55
430	3/ 30.04	3/ 30.53	3/ 31.02	3/ 31.50	3/ 31.99	3/ 32.48	3/ 32.97	3/ 33.46	3/ 33.95	3/ 34.44
440	3/ 34.93	3/ 35.42	3/ 35.91	3/ 36.40	3/ 36.89	3/ 37.38	3/ 37.87	3/ 38.36	3/ 38.85	3/ 39.34
450	3/ 39.83	3/ 40.32	3/ 40.81	3/ 41.30	3/ 41.79	3/ 42.28	3/ 42.77	3/ 43.25	3/ 43.74	3/ 44.23
460	3/ 44.72	3/ 45.21	3/ 45.70	3/ 46.19	3/ 46.68	3/ 47.17	3/ 47.66	3/ 48.15	3/ 48.64	3/ 49.13
470	3/ 49.62	3/ 50.11	3/ 50.60	3/ 51.09	3/ 51.58	3/ 52.07	3/ 52.56	3/ 53.05	3/ 53.54	3/ 54.03
480	3/ 54.52	3/ 55.00	3/ 55.49	3/ 55.98	3/ 56.47	3/ 56.96	3/ 57.45	3/ 57.94	3/ 58.43	3/ 58.92
490	3/ 59.41	3/ 59.90	4/ .39	4/ .88	4/ 1.37	4/ 1.86	4/ 2.35	4/ 2.84	4/ 3.33	4/ 3.82
500	4/ 4.31	4/ 4.80	4/ 5.29	4/ 5.78	4/ 6.27	4/ 6.75	4/ 7.24	4/ 7.73	4/ 8.22	4/ 8.71
510	4/ 9.20	4/ 9.69	4/ 10.18	4/ 10.67	4/ 11.16	4/ 11.65	4/ 12.14	4/ 12.63	4/ 13.12	4/ 13.61
520	4/ 14.10	4/ 14.59	4/ 15.08	4/ 15.57	4/ 16.06	4/ 16.55	4/ 17.04	4/ 17.53	4/ 18.02	4/ 18.50
530	4/ 18.99	4/ 19.48	4/ 19.97	4/ 20.46	4/ 20.95	4/ 21.44	4/ 21.93	4/ 22.42	4/ 22.91	4/ 23.40
540	4/ 23.89	4/ 24.38	4/ 24.87	4/ 25.36	4/ 25.85	4/ 26.34	4/ 26.83	4/ 27.32	4/ 27.81	4/ 28.30
550	4/ 28.79	4/ 29.28	4/ 29.77	4/ 30.25	4/ 30.74	4/ 31.23	4/ 31.72	4/ 32.21	4/ 32.70	4/ 33.19
560	4/ 33.68	4/ 34.17	4/ 34.66	4/ 35.15	4/ 35.64	4/ 36.13	4/ 36.62	4/ 37.11	4/ 37.60	4/ 38.09
570	4/ 38.58	4/ 39.07	4/ 39.56	4/ 40.05	4/ 40.54	4/ 41.03	4/ 41.52	4/ 42.00	4/ 42.49	4/ 42.98
580	4/ 43.47	4/ 43.96	4/ 44.45	4/ 44.94	4/ 45.43	4/ 45.92	4/ 46.41	4/ 46.90	4/ 47.39	4/ 47.88
590	4/ 48.37	4/ 48.86	4/ 49.35	4/ 49.84	4/ 50.33	4/ 50.82	4/ 51.31	4/ 51.80	4/ 52.29	4/ 52.78

Another page from Project Tempo, this time with videotape. Notice that it is expressed in minutes and seconds.

Diagram 8

an electronic device called a click track exists for the purpose of assuring accuracy in rhythm. By using this method, an arranger or composer can determine with great accuracy just where any given visual cue will fall within the composition.

In the recording studio, the music producer will undoubtedly want to check his musical score against the picture. This is almost always true in a post-score situation. He can then determine whether or not any adjustments have to be made, or if he made any errors in his layout of the music. (Yes, even with click there can be mistakes.) A well-equipped recording studio should have the proper facilities so that you can watch the picture as you play back the audio track. This is most often accomplished before the recording session by transferring your film to a professional videotape cassette and then using that as your playback system for your picture. This video cassette is similar to a Betamax or VHS system used by consumers, but is considerably larger.

Sound on Film vs. Sound on Videotape

A :60 commercial actually has only fifty-eight seconds of audio. A :30 commercial uses twenty-eight seconds of audio, and a :10 spot uses eight seconds of audio. This is because the method used to "read" sound by the movie projector prohibits the sound track from being in line with the film. The "sound head" (playback head) of the film projector is displaced from the "gate" (projection lens) (see diagram 9). This means that if two pieces of film were spliced together using only the last frame of picture for reference, you would cut off the end part of the audio track from film #1. Here's why:

Film is *pulled* through a projector's gate frame by frame. This is called a sprocket drive. If you slowed down the film projector you would see that a gate opens and closes (twenty-four times per second) to illuminate one frame of film at a time. At full speed the picture seems continuous, even though it is actually a series of jerky movements. Therefore the sound head that is needed to read the audio track, which is encoded on the edge of the film, had to be put somewhere else along the film's path through the projector. This playback system is actually located *after* the lens, which means that the sound track is in a different place from the frame of picture that it matches. In this way it can be located at a point where the film's movement is smooth and unencumbered. Study the diagram of the projector if you have trouble understanding this point and notice that the lens and the sound head are in two totally different places.

Tape recorders, on the other hand, use a continuous, smooth feed system, technically referred to as a capstan drive. There is no opening or closing of a gate or projection lens because there is no lens on a tape recorder.

Maybe the easiest way to understand this is to keep in mind that film has sprocket holes and that tape does not. Therefore the methods used to drive the film and "decode" the audio part of it are necessarily different from the method used to drive and "decode" audio tape.

Of the two, film is more precise. Tape has the ability to stretch or slip. Film, with its sprocket holes, maintains a constant speed.

Although a commercial may be presented to a television network on film, the network will actually transfer and then broadcast the spot on videotape. This enables the commercial to be easily cut into the network's regular programming. Videotape is also considered easier to handle than film,

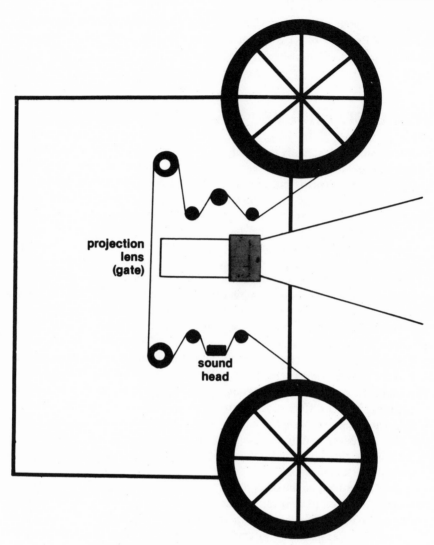

projection lens (gate)

sound head

Picture occurs at a different place than audio.

Diagram 9

and since the drive system for film is more complex and subject to problems, and film also breaks and tears easily, videotape tends to be more reliable.

Most major advertising agencies do this film-to-tape conversion before delivering the commercial to the network. There are exceptions to this, particularly on the local level, where film is still shipped to the station; but more and more, videotape has become the medium on which commercials are delivered.

If you are going to deliver your tape of the Crunchies commercial to the network(s) on videotape, you have an added advantage. You can now extend your audio track to a full thirty seconds! The problem that existed on film, where the sound head was displaced from the gate, no longer exists. On videotape sound and picture are encoded simultaneously in sync with each other. Some film editors like to leave up to a half-second at the top of the videotape before the audio starts. This is simply so that sound can be faded in quickly. It sounds nicer than starting the audio track abruptly. In day-to-day usage, however, most film editors leave $\frac{1}{3}$ second at the top and $\frac{1}{3}$ second at the tail. Again, this is so the commercial sounds smoother and less abrupt. This then allows you a total of twenty-nine and one-third seconds of audio on a commercial being delivered on videotape.

Let's review some of the basics about film and videotape that we've just discussed.

1. All professional film formats run at twenty-four (24) frames *per second*.
2. 35mm film has sixteen (16) frames *per foot*.
3. 16mm film has forty (40) frames *per foot*.
4. The sound-track length for a commercial being delivered to the station or network(s) on *film* is always two (2) seconds *shorter* than the visual. Therefore, a thirty-second commercial only has a twenty-eight-second audio track, etc.
5. The soundtrack length for a commercial being delivered to the station or network(s) on *videotape* is only $\frac{2}{3}$'s of a second shorter than the visual. Therefore, a thirty-second commercial has a twenty-nine-and-one-third ($29\frac{1}{3}$) second audio track.
6. Click track is a method of measuring and maintaining the different tempos of music in relation to the unvarying speed of film. It does this by measuring the amount of film that has passed through the gate for every beat of music. Click is expressed in eighths, i.e. a 13-5 click actually means $13\frac{5}{8}$ frames of film per beat of music.
7. Tape is capstan driven since it has no sprocket holes. Film is sprocket driven because it has sprocket holes.

Recording the Announcer

Let's assume that we have finished our music tracks but we still need to record the announcer reading copy for our Crunchies commercial. There are three ways to accomplish this:

First, we could use our multi-track recording (the 24-track) and insert the announcer onto an open track while we are at the recording session. Or, we could record the announcer on a separate piece of tape, if we know our time requirements exactly and know where we are going to insert it in the commercial. Our final option would be to record the announcer at the film-mix studio while he or she watches the film.

Each of these procedures has certain advantages. In our first example, if we record on the 24-track, we have the same kind of control over the announcer that we have over the music. Everything is automatically locked together and it is easy for both the engineer and the announcer to record, since only one machine has to be operated. It is very easy to play back music and announcer together since they are both on the same tape. In the final music mix, there is the additional advantage of being able to integrate the announcer right into the music track without any difficulty, since, again, the music and announcer are on the same piece of recording tape. If you were mixing a radio commercial where there would be no film mix, this is the ideal method for recording your announcer(s). Lastly, this method is the most economical, since there is no need for additional tape and only one machine is being operated during the recording and mix processes.

If we have already used up all of our tracks or if we are working with film, the second option is just as practical—to record the announcer on a separate piece of tape. This process is called recording "wild." When we combine all of the audio elements at the film mix, it is easier to have everything separate. We will be discussing this very point in just a little while.

A disadvantage of the above process is that to hear the announcer played back with the music, we would need to run *both* the multi-track tape and the tape machine that the announcer was recorded on. An advantage of this method is that you can save money by recording the announcer in a smaller voiceover studio rather than a larger and more expensive multi-track facility.

The advantage of the third method, recording at the film mix, is that it gives the announcer, who is probably also an actor or actress a chance to react to the film. This is particularly true if the announcer is supposed to be reacting to something specific that he or she will see on the screen but which might be hard to visualize by only reading a script in a recording studio.

The Technical Work of Combining Audio with Film

(A Discussion of "Full Coats" And "Stripes")

We have now completed all of our audio tracks, including the announcer, musicians, and singers. The only other possible audio tracks that we may still

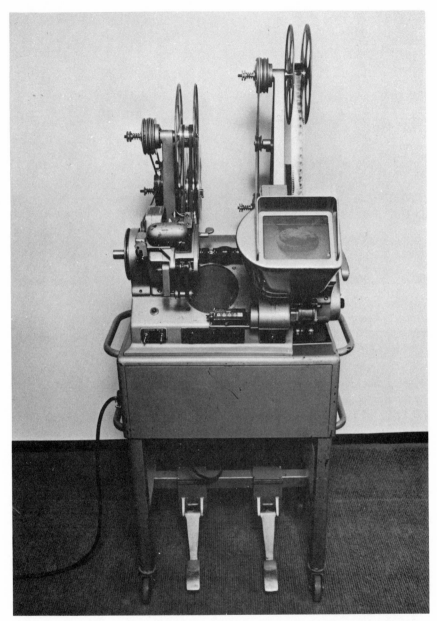

A Movieola, one of the most popular of all film editing machines. Notice that the film containing the picture is on the right and the mag containing the sound is on the left.

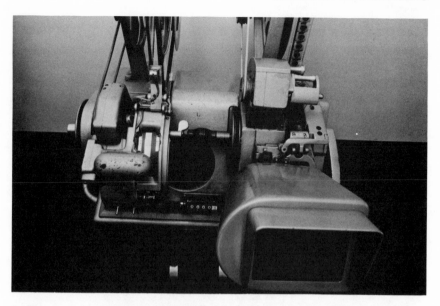

A close-up of a Movieola showing the soundhead on the left. Notice that a stripe is being used for the sound track. Also notice that one common drive shaft connects the picture with the sound track. That is why this is called an interlock.

wish to add are the all-important sound effects. These are usually assembled by the film editor, unless the sound effects are musical. We will discuss sound effects a bit later in this section. We now need to get our audio tracks into a form that is usable, i.e. compatible, with our film. If we have done our audio tracks as a pre-score procedure, before the actual filming of the commercial, the film editor will cut the film to the music on his Movieola, the most popular and commonly found machine used for editing film.

As we discussed, tape is capstan driven. This means that a pinch roller, which is a large rubber wheel, pushes up against a steel post. As the tape is fed through the roller and post, there is, as we said, some possibility of slippage and stretching. There is no way to accurately lock together the operating speed of a tape recorder and a film projector. (As we will see shortly, there *is* a way to lock together the speed of a tape recorder and a film *camera*.) Since film is the more complex medium, we must now adapt our audio tracks to the medium of film.

To do this, the audio track must be **dubbed** (transferred or copied) onto a special type of 35mm or 16mm film. This type of film is called a "mag" (magnetic transfer) and is put on the Movieola right alongside the picture. The audio is then lined up with the film. For the first time since we started

Here is another type of film editing machine called a "flatbed." Notice the stripe in the foreground for sound and the picture in the rear. The empty center reels allow for a second stripe. In this way an editor could listen to music on one stripe with sound effects on another.

recording our Crunchies commercial, the sound is "interlocked" with the picture. That is to say, it is locked in perfect sync with our picture. The interlock insures that the sound and picture are running at the same speed and starting at the same time.

At the film-mix studio the editor will put the film on a projector that is locked into sync with several sound dubbers. The dubbers play only the audio tracks. It is best to invite the music house composer-arranger to the final film mix to avoid any problems or to answer any possible questions about the sound or relative balances of the audio tracks.

There are two basic types of mags: **full coat** and a **stripe.** While reading this next section, look at the film samples inserted in the back pocket of this book. The full coat is the 35mm piece of film that is totally brown. The stripe is the 35mm piece of film that is clear with two brown stripes down either side.

Simply stated, a **mag,** whether a full coat or a stripe, is a length of 35mm film coated with recording oxide. This is the same material that is used on regular recording tape. A **full coat,** then, is a piece of 35mm film that is totally brown on one side because it is fully coated with recording oxide. The dull side is the oxide side, and is the one used for recording. A **stripe** is a

A modern dubbing room. The dubbers pictured are all *playback* dubbers. It is not unusual to use all of them during a complicated film mix.

mag with two thin, brown stripes, and like its cousin the full coat, has an oxide side and a shiny side. The wider of the two brown stripes is used for recording. The other brown stripe, the thinner one, is called a balance stripe. Without it the tape would be lopsided on its hub since one edge would be thicker than the other. The balance stripe is never used for recording.

Most of the time, to maintain the greatest flexibility at our upcoming film mix, the audio tracks for the music are not delivered as a final mono mix. Instead, they are supplied and delivered to the film editor as a multi-track element that contains *three* separate tracks: a full coat. So instead of mixing our Crunchies commercial to only a mono version at the final audio mix (the one you did at the recording studio) you also mix to a four-track tape recorder. It's really very simple and here's how it works.

Since we will be using a full coat at our film mix, we can separate the music into different sections. For instance, on one track of the four-track tape recorder you might have strings, brass, and woodwinds combined. The second track could have the entire rhythm section, while the third track contains the singer(s). The fourth track on the four-track tape recorder is used for recording a special sync signal. By using this sync signal while transferring the recording tape onto a mag, the speed of the tape can be regulated to keep it running exactly "on speed." (We'll discuss sync in a bit more detail later in this section.)

In using this four-track mix, any of the three sections—strings, rhythm, and singer—can be raised, lowered, or even omitted at the film mix. This gives us the flexibility to see our music with film *along with* the sound effects and announcer, if it was recorded separately, and to adjust the relative balances of each. With a mono mix, we would only have the option of taking the entire music track—strings, woodwinds, brass, singer(s), rhythm—and raising or lowering the whole thing as a unit. With a full coat we have the option of making only one element of the music louder or softer in relation to all of our other audio tracks. We could, for instance, make the rhythm section softer. We could raise the level (volume) of the singer in relation to the rest of the band. In other words, we still have a lot of control over the music, since we are using a full coat—a multi-track film element that contains three tracks of audio information—and not a straight mono mix.

A **stripe** is simply a mono mix. It is created on a two-track tape recorder. Like the full coat that was created on the four-track tape recorder, you need a separate track for the sync signal, so that everything keeps running at the proper speed. Therefore the mono mix goes on one track while the sync signal goes on the other. Since a stripe only has one piece of audio information, it would normally be used for an announcer or sound effects. Each different sound effect is usually on a separate stripe.

The film editor also uses a stripe of your music mix on his Movieola to start aligning picture and sound. This is because most Movieolas are not designed to play back all three tracks of a full coat. Therefore it is usually necessary to create both a full coat and a stripe at the recording studio. If you haven't done a separate mono mix, your recording engineer can do one easily by running a quick mix of the four-track to a mono. This is why you will occasionally hear a film editor refer to a stripe as a "mixed mag." They are simply referring to a full coat that has been mixed to mono and transferred to a stripe for their convenience in the editing room.

There is also another very clever use for a stripe. Assume that you have a special musical effect that you *don't* want included in your full coat because you're not sure how prominently it should be featured in the final sound track. If you included it in the music that's on the full coat you'd have no control over it, since it would be an integral part of whatever musical section it was included within.

Here's what to do. At the recording studio, do not include this effect or instrument or what-have-you in your mix to the four-track tape recorder, the one being used to create the full coat. Instead, transfer *just that track* from the 24-track tape recorder to the two-track tape recorder, the one used to create the stripe. Then you have that one instrument or sound totally separate and can make a decision at the film mix as to the level at which it will be featured. The sync signal will assure that it stays in sync with *both* the film and the full coat.

Remember that each mag goes onto a separate dubber. A dubber is a machine that records and plays back mags. Ten mags require ten dubbers. Don't go crazy with a zillion different mags, but do use as many as you need to maintain the flexibility you need in the film mix.

Let's review a few important points:

1. Announcers and other voiceovers can be recorded three different ways: directly onto the 24-track tape recorder, "wild" (onto a separate mono tape recorder), or live at the film mix.
2. A full coat is a mag (magnetic transfer) onto 35mm or 16mm film that is totally coated with recording oxide. In advertising a full coat contains three separate tracks.
3. A stripe is a mag onto 35mm or 16mm film that contains two brown stripes, only one of which is used for recording. A stripe contains only one track of audio information.
4. A dubber is a machine used to play back a mag.
5. Sync signal is encoded on one track of the four-track tape recorder for a full coat.
6. Sync signal is encoded on one track of the two-track tape recorder for a stripe.

Sync Signal

Sync is a 60-cycle signal that is used to keep the tape running at perfect speed. The electricity that comes out of the wall socket in the United States is 60 cycle. This 60-cycle system also governs the speed of clocks, radios, food processors—virtually all our electrical appliances. Since this 60 cycles never varies, we use it as a benchmark. The sync signal that we encode on our audio tape of the Crunchies commercial is necessary to keep the recording tape running exactly at the proper speed. This is essential for the making of a full coat or stripe. The recording tape with the sync signal is then fed through a machine called a **resolver.** The resolver is electronically connected to the tape recorder when we want to make a mag. The 60-cycle signal forces the tape machine to operate at a constant speed, even if the tape is slipping or stretching a bit. If the resolver senses that the 60-cycle signal, which should also be *playing back* at 60 cycles, has dropped to, lets say, 57 cycles, it causes the machine to run faster. If it senses the recorded signal at 63 cycles, it causes the machine to slow down. This is all accomplished by a special playback head installed on the tape recorder *ahead* of the normal head assembly that we described in the section entitled "The Recording Studio." It reads and interprets the sync signal *before* the regular material (music, announcer, sound effects) gets to the playback head.

During the final audio mix at the recording studio, the track that contains the sync signal on the 24-track machine is patched directly to the 4-track and 2-track tape recorders (see diagram 10). The same sync signal used to record the original music is placed on the 4- and 2-track tape recorders, giving us maximum accuracy. If our timings were correct on the 24-track they should also be correct, in fact identical, on the 4- and 2-track. Remember, once the audio tape has been transferred to a mag, the sync signal is *no longer necessary,* since a mag is sprocket driven. Therefore the full coat has only *three* tracks on it, even though the tape used to create it had four.

Pilotone

In pre-score situations where there is to be playback of the audio track on the set, we usually use a small portable, and very accurate tape recorder called a Nagra. The tape copy (dub) that we give the sound technician to be played back on the Nagra must be encoded with a different type of sync called **pilotone.** This keeps the Nagra running at the correct speed in much the same way a resolver keeps a tape recorder running at the correct speed while making a mag. After the film editor receives the processed film, he will use a stripe of the sound track to help him align audio and picture. The editor's stripe will have been made with a mono mix encoded with 60-cycle sync. Remember, this mix was created on a 2-track tape recorded with the mono mix of our music on one track and 60-cycle sync on the other. This is the same mix that the pilotone transfer was created from, and therefore everything will appear in sync.

Both authors have had painful experiences where there was a slip-up by someone in the sync process. It is a real horror story when it is impossible to match lip movements with the music track because a non-pilotone copy was used on the set or because someone used a non-sync tape mix to create the mag. This is one area where you should pay close attention to detail.

Let your sound technician know that you are supplying a pilotone copy of the sound track. If he doesn't ''see'' the pilotone on his meters, don't shoot film until the situation is resolved (no pun intended). An agency producer should let the assistant director (AD) know that sync copies do indeed exist. This way everyone is looking out for any possible errors.

Which to Use: Full Coat or Stripe

Sound effects are usually supplied as stripes and not full coats, so that they are more easily moved forward or backward for adjustment to the film. As a general rule, music is the only element supplied as a full coat.

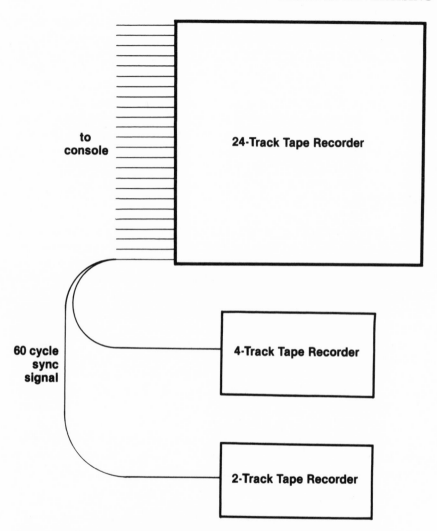

Sync signal gets patched directly from the 24-track to both the 4-track and 2-track machines during a final mix.

Diagram 10

As we said before, a good film facility has as many as ten or more dubbers. If you are working on a complicated piece of film that requires a lot of audio elements, be sure that your film studio can handle them. This is particularly true when you are working outside a major production center.

If you are working in a studio that doesn't have enough dubbers, you can combine your stripes into an additional full coat. In a smaller facility this procedure could save your mix session and make you look like quite a knowledgeable producer. In a larger facility you might have to do this if machinery is out of order.

A good film-mix engineer is hard to find. He or she has to be able to achieve the perfect balance between music, picture, sound effects, announcer, and action. Because of the large number of elements involved, this is a more complex process than working with sound alone. Because of its complexity, a very small number of film mixers do the bulk of the work. It is a very specialized job.

So that you understand each step in its proper sequence, let's review the studio process from the time a commercial is created until it is ready to be mixed. In the example below, the music was written before the film was shot, a pre-score situation.

1. Agency conceives a commercial.
2. Agency contacts several music houses and listens to demos.
3. Agency chooses a music house to do the commercial.
4. Music composer and agency producer discuss lyrics, key points of the commercial, possibly the use of announcer and sound effects.
5. Composer writes a demo and presents it to the agency. This may be a more finished version of the piano or guitar demo originally submitted.
6. Agency approves demo.
7. Recording session takes place where the music and singers are recorded.
8. The film is shot to the music.
9. The film editor, together with the agency, decides what shots to use and assembles them. The film is then taken to a film-mix facility where the music, announcer, sound effects, and whatever other audio tracks are being used will be combined in a final mix.

If the film were shot *before* the music was done, you would go through these steps only after the film has been edited to a rough cut and the composer and arranger could take their timings.

The Final Mix: Combining Audio and Film

At this point you probably have a full coat of music, a stripe or two of sound effects, and a stripe or two of announcer copy. Our film-mix engineer (film mixer) needs to look at the picture and listen to all of the audio tracks *individually* to get some idea of what is on each track. The audio console is sort of a miniature version of the audio console at the recording session.

A modern film-mix facility with the projection screen on the left and the console on the right. Also notice the small TV that permits you to hear and see your spot immediately on TV after you finish mixing.

Give your film mixer five minutes or so to work on the various tracks without any interference. When he or she starts to get a rough balance of the various full coats and stripes, you can begin to comment on which aspects of the sound you want to stress. The film editor has handed your engineer a very lengthy cue sheet that breaks down all of the various cues in your commercial (see diagram 11). You need to maintain your perspective on which elements of sound are important, and what needs to be stressed, glossed over, or even omitted. Be sure to listen to the audio portion on a small speaker, just as it will be heard on television. At this point you will be unable to decide that you don't like a guitar part, or that you want to experiment with the basic sound. Film-mix studios are busy places, and they are usually pretty strict about runover time. But more important, the time to make changes has come and gone. This is the time to combine everything. The experimentation should have occurred with your film editor at his or her office and with your music producer at the original recording session.

In this final film mix we are combining all full coats and stripes to yet another full coat. This new full coat would typically have one track of the music, which would now be totally combined as a mono mix, another track of announcer, actors and actresses, and one track of sound effects. We are recording directly onto mag now, so there is no need for sync, since the machine that is recording this new mag is locked into the same drive system

A close-up of a film-mix console from the engineer's vantage point, looking out towards the projection screen. Notice that a podium has been set up for an announcer to be able to record the copy while looking at the picture. Also notice that the console is smaller and more limited in capabilities than the one shown in the recording studio.

as the other dubbers. In fact, the only real difference is that the dubber with the new full coat is recording while the other dubbers are only playing back already recorded tracks. At a later date your film *editor* will see to it that this new full coat is combined to a mono mix.

The reason for not going to a final mono mix at this time is once again to gain the versatility of being able to rebalance one element against the other, even after you have left the studio! For instance, if you return to the office and decide that the announcer is too low, you can simply call the film editor and have him run another mix with the announcer's volume up a bit. There is no need for you to be there, since the music and effects have already been mixed correctly (see diagram 12).

In a videotape mix, all sound is combined on a monaural audio track. This is somewhat easier than mixing to a full coat, but the same basic decisions remain. Videotapes do not normally use mags because you are not working with film. Tape transfers are easier because the equipment used is easier to work with than film equipment. In some of the newer mixing facilities, the film is transferred to videotape to speed up the rewinding process, and thus speed the film mix.

At this stage of our mix everything is interlocked: sound effects, an-

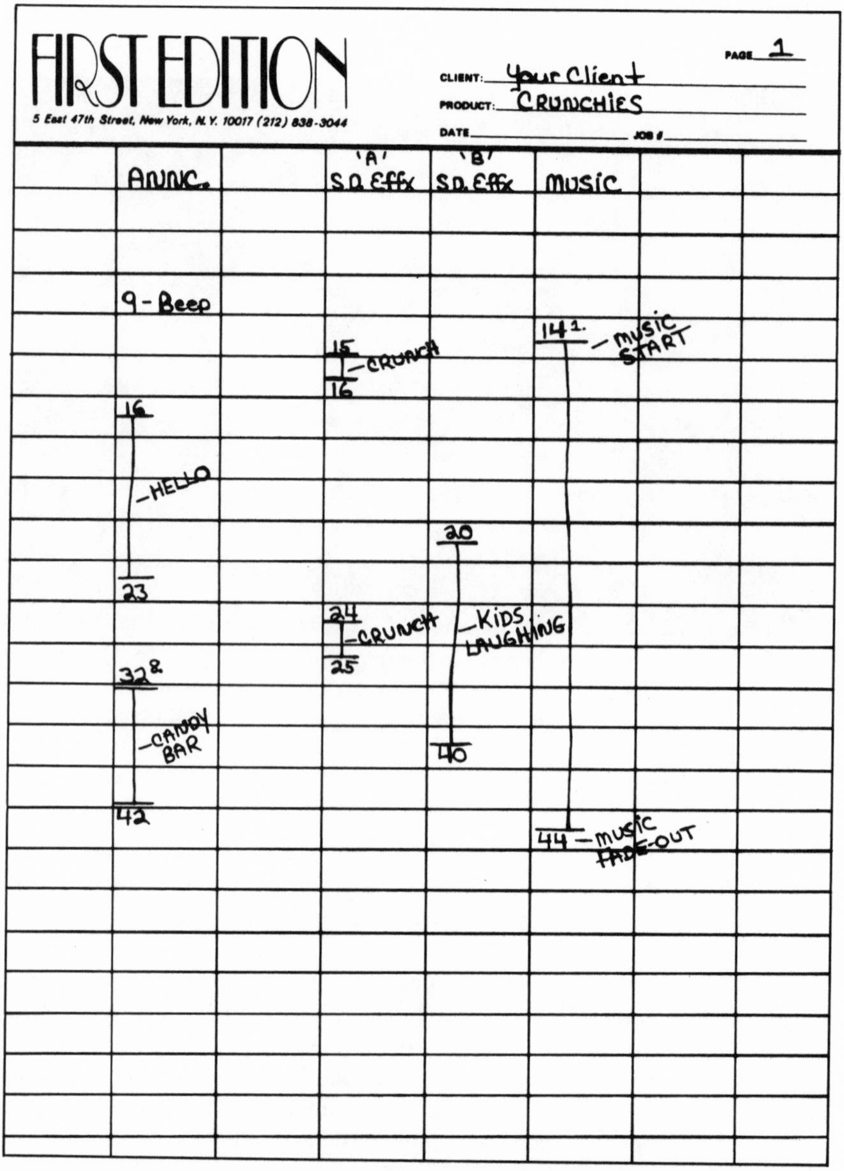

The above cue sheet is for our Crunchies spot. The numbers refer to footage counts for 35mm film. Notice that music starts at 14 feet, 1 frame in from what is known as the "start mark". This is a mark that the editor places on the film and mags to line them up in sync with each other. This mark always occurs 12 feet ahead of the first frame of picture.

Diagram 11

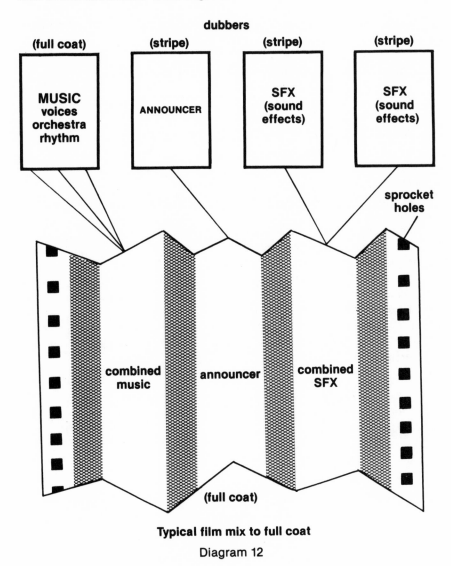

Typical film mix to full coat

Diagram 12

nouncer, music, and vocals. Everything is synchronized to the film. Our final mix is now complete. We then show the finished commercial to the client and get final approval. If everything is satisfactory, we can advise our film editor that it is a "buy." If the relative balances are not acceptable, you can usually re-mix the newly created full coat to obtain a satisfactory balance and go through the approval process one more time.

Let's briefly review the process of combining the finished audio tracks and picture.

1. The film editor is supplied with both a stripe and a full coat of the music tracks by the music house or music producer. The editor is also supplied with stripes of any other special effects, sound effects, and announcer tracks he requires.
2. The editor aligns all of the elements (mags) so that music, sound effects, etc. all fall in the proper places.
3. The film mixer combines all of the different elements (mags) onto one final full coat.
4. You play the finished commercial for the agency and your client, Crunchies.
5. Any adjustments to the sound track are made. Step 4 is then repeated.
6. The film editor finishes whatever additional visual effects (opticals) are needed and shows the client and agency the final picture.
7. The finished commercial is then either transferred to videotape for delivery to the station(s) or network(s), or final film prints for shipment to the station(s) or network(s) are authorized.
8. The campaign is a smash. Brilliant agency personnel get raises, receive vice presidencies, and make gracious acceptance speeches at awards ceremonies.

PART THREE

The Uses of Audio in Advertising

How Music and Sound Enhance a Commercial

Now that we have covered studio procedures and the integration of music, spoken words, sound effects, and picture, it is appropriate that we discuss what lies behind the *use* of sound in commercials. There are many books that describe the theory and practice of advertising in general, and it is not our purpose to review that material.

A good commercial creates or helps to expand the image of the product. "See the USA in your Chevrolet" says one thing when viewed in a newspaper advertisement. It is another creature entirely when the words are spoken by a professional spokesperson. When music is added we have the icing on the cake—a slogan that can be sung, hummed, and more easily remembered. The consumer's recall of the product may occur independently of any particular event or phenomenon, or it may come to mind as our target population thinks of buying a car, passes the showroom of a car dealer, or just sees a Chevy driving along the road.

Music in a commercial is also entertainment. Many of the soft drink commercials are very much like pop records—catchy, memorable, and easy on the ear. They are intended to create an image built around the product, while other campaigns are designed to reinforce an idea that has already been promoted. "Things go better with Coke" didn't really break any new ground, it simply reminded the public that Coke and good times were synonymous. Bell Telephone's campaign for long-distance calls was designed to tell us to "reach out." Friends are only a phone call away, no matter how many miles may separate you from them.

Music can also help gain access to your precise demographics. A hard-rock commercial is designed to zero in on the ten-to-twenty-five-year-old segment of the population. Remember the 7-Up commercials where the product was referred to as "the un-Cola"? Almost all of the music was heavy metal rock combined with some very innovative graphics. 7-Up knew who they were after and they went after them with a vengeance. This commercial was a wonderful example of visuals and audio working so well together that the campaign was long lived and very effective. Even when it was adapted to radio, the music was still effective because it was constantly reinforced with TV, print, and billboard.

Miller Beer is still another example. The closing billboard, "If you've got the time, we've got the beer" is an outstanding example of well-produced music constantly updating the image of the product. Rather than run the identical piece of music behind each spot, new openings to each commercial feature a different visual and different music. The only common denominator is the end billboard lyric and melody. Miller knows who its audience is, and customizes the entire campaign to them.

Avoiding Music

Miller Lite is yet another example. There is no musical theme in these commercials, yet they are among the most effective beer commercials on the air today. They are aimed at the sports market, who might have thought that a "lite" beer would be too sissy for them. But by designing a campaign around macho sports celebrities and letting them appear doing some jock humor, the beer is given a credibility that it might not otherwise have. Also, listen to how well the sound effects on the Miller Lite spots are handled. The setting always creates the ambience of a fun place to be.

In the movie *Fail-Safe,* Sidney Lumet decided that he wanted to create the maximum shock value by having the film seem as real as possible. In *Fail-Safe* there is not *one* note of music. The effect is really devastating. So remember that music may not always be the vehicle to tell your story. It wasn't for Sidney Lumet and it wasn't for Miller Lite. On the other hand, it is hard to imagine Coke, Pepsi, Burger King, or McDonalds without it.

More Uses of Music

A good music track establishes a certain sense of locale. Every form of music has its own paraphernalia and ambience—musicians in a string quartet are expected to look formal, dressing in tuxedos or gowns. They bespeak an evening of formality, a certain refinement. A commercial that is supposed to appeal to truck drivers has a whole other look and sound, and part of that is reinforced by the music. We have steel guitars and cowboy hats instead of violins and tuxedos, banjos and jeans instead of cellos and gowns.

Sometimes we are trying to create a *less* specific or obvious mood through the use of sophisticated audio and visual techniques. This sort of sales message is more subtle and intuitive, based on feelings rather than a clear and simple sales pitch. The Bell System's corporate advertising highlighting its newest technology is a great example of this type of approach.

Initiating A Campaign

A successful campaign begins with intelligent planning on the part of the agency and the client. We need to know what it is we are trying to sell, and who the audience is that is going to buy. When Ron Lockhart was hired to do the music for Stanley Tools, the company had decided that they wanted to reach the consumer market for tools—the amateur handyman. So the logo "Stanley, we want to help you do things right" was created and was backed up with booklets given away at the point of purchase, which indeed showed the amateur how to do many common jobs around the house. The same campaign line and music is still running, and the effect has been exactly what Stanley Tools wanted. They have received a greater share of their market and their visibility and credibility are enhanced.

A commercial can certainly be used to transform the image of a product. *The New Yorker* print and radio ads were designed to show that the magazine was alive and vibrant and not the stuffy publication that most people visualized. The emphasis was placed on what is in *The New Yorker* now, as opposed to what the consumer might guess was there. In this case, part of the design of the campaign was directed squarely at their competition, *New York Magazine*.

Several years ago, another magazine came out with a great slogan and aired it all over the radio and then reinforced it in print. The slogan was "*Look* is bigger than life." The double entendre was intentional and the effect of that spot was quite long lived.

The spoken word can also help to build product identity. Dick and Burt, Bob and Ray, and Stan Freberg are among the most successful creators of humorous audio advertisements that have helped to create product images. Their work is always entertaining to the public, which tends to draw attention away from the fact that the message is a commercial one. Bob and Ray's Piel's beer spots, and the *Time* commercials by Dick and Burt have all helped to establish product identities. The Stiller and Mera Blue Nun wine commercials had a specific purpose, but they were also quite entertaining. The idea being communicated was that wine should be part of a meal, not a luxury for the upper classes. Today, that ad might seem out of place, since wine is more universally accepted among Americans. Might the Blue Nun commercials be partly responsible for that phenomenon?

Developing a Campaign

A good campaign needs a focal point for the music or spoken words. An idea could be anything, but it must prove sufficiently interesting to attract the attention of the consumer. One of the worst mistakes in advertising is to bombard the viewer or listener with too many ideas, so that when the commercial is over there is no clear memory of what has been said. Pacing and liveliness are part of an effective message, and on TV there are so many variables between the sound and picture that without simplicity of concept, clarity may be difficult to achieve.

The initial phase of a campaign with music (specifically a jingle) might go something like this. The spots would air with the full lyric version. After this had been run and proved effective, a donut version would be prepared. In the donut version, copy is inserted in the middle of the commercial. Usually the music is played quietly behind the announcer copy. The final phase of a campaign might include just the billboard or product logo—"Stanley, we want to help you do things right." By the time the billboard phase has been reached, the public should be able to recognize the product and the jingle. This effect is achieved through constant repetition, adequate time buys, and because the campaign is sufficently appealing to be memorable. Visual aids are still another level of product image. The Schlitz Malt Liquor bull, Mr. Goodwrench, and Madge the manicurist are but three examples of this.

It is *very, very* important to realize that television, radio, print, and billboard are all entirely different media. A great TV spot may not work on radio because of the importance of the visual aspects of the commercial. On radio the audio portion of a commercial is everything, while in television the variables and action are far more complex.

Certain DJ's and announcers are particularly adept at inserting product messages into the regular format of their shows, usually in a humorous way. A long-time sponsor on a particular radio program is very likely to get kidded and joked about on the air. Usually, the client and the agency are ecstatic about this kind of visibility (or should we say audibility) and treatment. This attention can be requested by the agency, particularly when the copy is to be performed by the live announcer and has not been pre-recorded. Johnny Carson occasionally does the same thing on *The Tonight Show,* or he kids Ed McMahon about Budweiser or the Alpo dog. Why do you think Alpo and Budweiser keep including *The Tonight Show* in their media buys?

Stock and Library Music

If you are under a severe budget limitation, it is possible to purchase stock or library music. This is music recorded by musicians, often overseas to avoid residuals. It is designed to fit specific moods or tempos, and one example might be: a 30-second segment of country fiddle music. This music is not tailored to your particular product, but is intended to fit in a more general way. It is also used over and over again in different markets or for different products. In fact, much music is used on a national or network basis (these terms are synonomous) and can be heard on different sponsors' advertisement during the same program! This, to understate the matter, causes a vague familiarity to the listener, something like one's reaction to hearing an old song on Muzak at your dentist's office.

The music in a car commercial aired in Denver may also have been heard on stations in Santa Fe and Cheyenne advertising other brands of cars or even a local furniture store. This sort of commercial is called a **drop-in.** A drop-in unlike library music, is personalized in the clients name. A drop-in uses an old instrumental track with a new vocal track, inserted in place of the old client.

Library music usually has no lyrics. It is often distributed by the owner to the music houses, which act as distributors, on long-playing records. Each use of the music track is referred to as a "needle drop."

There is one advantage to the drop-in or needle drop: they are cheap to purchase or license. Their effectiveness, however, is open to debate. In a very small, insulated market, a drop-in is probably the best answer to what is essentially an economic problem. But once the stakes start getting bigger, when the clients are large chains of lumber yards, large department stores that advertise regionally, or, say, a chain of restaurants, drop-in's are self-defeating. Drop-in's by their very nature are not specific in terms of creating image. A client who has a significant media schedule and is spending significant dollars on air time and back-up print campaigns deserves something better than second-hand music. Certainly the authors of this book have a vested interest in saying this, but simply stated, it is foolish to be spending big bucks in media time to advertise and not put your best foot forward.

In our opinion, it is close to suicidal to run a *national* spot using stock music. It should be the agency's job to explain to its client that while the short-term goal of saving money may be realized, the long-term effects of product credibility and sales will most likely be harmed.

Technically, drop-ins and needle drops are illegal for any signatory to any of the performing union's agreements, because if they were recorded in the United States, there would have to be a new session fee paid to the musicians every time a new lyric was inserted or every time it was coupled with a new piece of film, whether or not it was for the same client. To our knowledge, this is not done. If the music is recorded in Europe, a violation of the AFM agreement has occurred, since as a signatory to the AFM agreement you have guaranteed not to record overseas.

The obvious motive is to save residuals, and there is no question that using drop-ins or library music accomplishes this. Whether or not it is as effective as original music, however, is another story entirely. If something is worth doing, it is worth doing right. Library music and drop-ins are, at best, compromises that detract from the effectiveness of your commercial. Originality is lost, the ability to have a customized billboard or tag is lost, and the end result is that the product suffers. Studies tend to support the view that effective advertising is more dependent on the image it creates than on the number of times it is played. Original music or clever use of audio are great image makers. Library music isn't an image maker at all.

It is also illegal to use hit records as background music to commercials, even though this is a very common practice in smaller markets. Larger products lease the rights to use hit songs for particular campaigns. To do so, they must pay a handsome fee to the publishers and/or record companies that wrote and performed the original music and control the rights. The composition "This Land Is Your Land," composed by Woody Guthrie, has appeared in a number of commercials, because it is a good vehicle for suggesting strong American locales and values." Up, Up and Away," used by TWA, is another example. But if the agency wished to use the *original* record version of that composition they would have to pay a licensing fee to the record company, a new session fee to the musicians and singers, make special compensation arrangements with the artist, and obtain a mechanical license from the music publisher, which permits the coupling of the music with the commercial. You can see why people almost never go to this trouble!

Nevertheless, all over the country, the actual records, not just the melody, are being used as background music for advertising. On radio this practice is particularly flagrant. However, since there is no easy way to police this abuse in local markets, it continues unabated.

Scoring and Music Arranging

Some music houses specialize in the instrumental scoring of commercials rather than commercials that involve singing. Singing commercials as we have noted before, are usually referred to as jingles. Scoring tends to be less intrusive and usually more subtle than a commercial involving lyrics. This may be the effect that you want for your particular product. It is also a bit cheaper than using singing commercials because the residuals for musicians are much less expensive than the repayment fees for singers. The creative fees for scoring also tend to be lower than the creative fees charged for jingles.

A creative instrumental that represents your product can do the same thing for the product image that a jingle with a full lyric can accomplish. The Marlboro cigarette theme was a classic example. The music, which was the original theme from the movie *The Magnificent Seven,* was just the thing for a cigarette ad that was trying to appeal to a youthful market.

A good music arranger can take a tune and use it in a variety of ways during the course of a musical campaign. We cannot give you any set criteria for selecting a tune that will lend itself to different sorts of musical arrangements, but your music house should be able to provide you with some examples of how a tune can be changed or rearranged. For example, if you have a middle-of-the-road sort of jingle, ask your music house to show you how it can be adapted to a Country & Western (C&W) or jazz format, or whatever else you might like to hear. A good arranger can make slight or extensive alterations in the musical character of a particular piece that will enable your jingle to adapt to different musical styles. These changes might include changing the time signature of your composition (from 4/4 to 3/4, for example), using different instrumentation (electric guitars instead of violins), altering a tempo, changing the vocalist or the overall vocal style (The Carpenters vs. The Eagles). Any or all of these changes can drastically alter the basic feel of the original commercial, just as in our earlier example of Miller Beer, where the billboard stays essentially the same but the opening of each commercial is completely different. Occasionally a melody is so locked in to a particular musical style that it is difficult, if not impossible, to rearrange the melody in another way. "The Star-Spangled Banner" would not make a good disco commercial, although it might sound pretty good in a soul version.

Budgets

You should be aware of some of the budgetary procedures relating to the use of music houses. Some music houses charge low fees for their creative work, but they insist that the composer appear on the AFTRA or SAG contract as a singer or actor regardless of whether he or she sings on or appears in the commercial. They consider this part of their compensation. In this way the composer gets to share in the healthy residuals that singers are paid for the re-use of the commercial, especially on a spot that is primarily aired **network** (nationally). This is not an uncommon practice among the top composers and producers in the industry. Often, in fact, the composers and/or producers really do sing on the commercial and will accept this as their additional compensation. Others insist that they be paid *twice:* once for singing on the commercial and once as a continuing licensing fee for the composition. This is not out of the ordinary, but it is considered somewhat extravagant.

Other music houses charge very high creative fees but do not insist on participation in residuals. This requires a pretty hefty allotment of money for production in your original budget, but if your spot is to air primarily network, you may save money in the long run.

The hottest composers and producers might well demand both high creative fees and participation in residuals. It is up to you to find out the details of the deal *before* you go into studio, not after. Nothing is more embarrassing than discovering, after the commercial is completed, that you still have to list the composer on the "contract" for his additional compensation and that your client has not counted on those monies in his budget.

A hot music house will never come cheap. In fact a really good music house with a consistent record of quality and success, even without the visibility of a lot of national spots, can be very costly. As in other aspects of advertising or life, you generally get what you pay for when you are buying a highly specialized service. Cheaper is usually not better, even though paying top dollar doesn't guarantee success. Remember to listen to the sample reels of music houses carefully. If a music house is good and they've been in business for several years, you are going to get a top-notch job. Casting the right music house for your job is ultimately your responsibility.

In a similar way, your goals for a particular commercial should govern the question of whether you will use professional voiceover talent or whether you want to rely on a disc jockey or announcer doing live announcer copy. The decision as to which alternative is preferable depends upon the talent involved and an understanding of your goals. If you need to save money, then by all means do so. It is part of your job to deliver to your client the job they need at a price they can afford. But do it with a clear understanding of what you may be giving up in trade for saving a few dollars.

An Overview of Problems and Possibilities

It seems fitting to end this book with a look at some of the problems that opened it. Let's take another look at pre-production as a tool for saving time and money and developing a better campaign. Particularly early in your career, when things are still new to you, the more you think out your market, the product image, and what you are trying to accomplish with a particular spot or campaign, the better off you are going to be in dealing with your music or audio team. What is the age, sex, income, and lifestyle of your target group? What kind of entertainment do they enjoy? Where do they live? And what are their habits, jobs, and aspirations? Almost all clients have a pretty good idea of their market by the research they have done. Be sure to use it.

Once that is accomplished, start working with your music producer and composer on a strong lyric that best expresses the product image. Remember, don't try to write a lyric if you don't know how, or if someone else can do it better. To be able to delegate authority is the true mark of a professional. Make sure that you exercise supervision over the actual content of the lyric and melody, making certain that it expresses the proper selling points for your campaign.

By all means let the music house develop the music, but you should research the musical styles that go with the demographics for this particular product. Do you want the commercial to sound more or less like a particular product, i.e., soft drink or fast food? Do you want the commercial to sound like a particular artist or group? You might want to consult *Billboard,* the primary music industry trade paper, to see what is hot on the charts at the moment. While advertising usually lags behind innovative musical styles, it does so only by a few months. Most campaigns take that long just to finish production and reach the air. A spot that goes into production in February but isn't going to air until October could easily adapt the current hot musical style if a contemporary sound is what you had in mind. Nothing is worse than giving a direction to a music house and being dissatisfied with the results because you didn't really know what a specific musical style was all about. In other words, if you asked for a Nashville sound, don't tell your music producer that you don't want to hear steel guitar or banjos.

Be aware of any difficulties that could occur in singing the lyrics for your commercial. It is difficult to hold out or sustain certain sounds. Some product names don't easily trip off a singer's tongue. Therefore, don't get committed to key selling points that are difficult to sing. Analyze what your competition is doing in terms of their selling points on similar products. Do you want to be in that same general area, or do you have some unique selling points that make your product stand out? A good campaign needs a combination of good commercials in the media you will be using, smart time buys for radio and TV, and a legitimate product strength. Good advertising may get someone to try a rotten product once, but you can bet they won't come back for more. If any aspect of the total picture is missing, there is a good chance that the final result will not justify your work.

Be sure that you are not telling too many stories—lyrically, musically, or visually—in a single commercial. The star of your commercial is the *product,* not the announcer, the music, or the visuals. The point of the campaign is always to sell the product or gain increased favorable visibility for your client. If a celebrity lends credibility to your product, this will certainly help you sell the product, especially if that celebrity is used wisely.

Robert Young is the spokesperson for Sanka coffee. Because of his association with the TV character Dr. Marcus Welby, there is a credibility to Mr. Young telling us that we'll feel better and be less jumpy if we drink Sanka.

O.J. Simpson for Hertz is another example. Mr. Simpson's image is that of a winner. Who wouldn't want to drive a car rented from a company that is represented by a man who is a famous athlete and film star?

Just be sure to use celebrity endorsements as carefully as you would anything else in the production of your commercial.

Lastly, your role in the studio is to supervise the overall production and to make sure that a commercial is achieving the maximum effectiveness for your product. When you listen to the audio mixes, make sure that the overall sound is what you want, that all lyrics are clearly audible, and that the feel of the music is what you and the composer had planned. Try not to mix a sound track to fit your boss's tastes. Rather, trust your instincts and do what you think is right. Many a spot has been ruined and many an agency employee has looked foolish by trying to second-guess what the boss will think. If you're good—and after all you *are* a professional—arrive at a finished mix that you like and can readily defend.

Always try to have a clear grasp of your goals. Generally, commercials are not the place to use revolutionary musical techniques. Rather, they should be the place to use creative versions of what the public has already been exposed to in other contexts. Dick Weissman has an unforgettable experience of watching Dick Clark's *American Bandstand* when it was on the air. Clark played the new record releases and asked teenagers in attendance to rate the records on a numerical scale of 100. During the show in question, Clark played a new record and a teenager he was questioning gave the record a 67, a rather low rating. Clark asked why he didn't like the record. The teenager was uncommunicative. He wouldn't say whether his dislike of the record was due to a poor beat, a bad singer, or whatever. Finally, Clark leaned over with a sly smile and asked if the reason that the fellow didn't like the record was because it was a "bit different." The boy instantly brightened. "Yes, that was it. It was too different!"

It is wonderful to use the intelligence and creativity of your talent and the technical expertise of your production crew to deliver a brilliant campaign. Just don't make it so different that no one understands or likes it. The only meaningful test for your work is whether it increases sales for the product. While that may sound unnecessarily harsh, this is, afterall, the advertising industry and *not* the record business. If it doesn't increase sales, or if it doesn't enhance the client's image (as in some corporate advertising), the campaign ultimately is a failure.

Your suppliers are your lifeblood in executing your ideas. They ultimately create what you have conceived, so remember to reward those who helped you with your successes and to replace those who failed. May the same thing happen to you!

GLOSSARY

Glossary

AFM American Federation of Musicians—the musicians' union.

AFTRA American Federation of Television and Radio Artists—the union that controls actors, announcers, and singers for radio and videotape commercials. The sister union to SAG.

Arranger A musician who writes the parts that each individual musician in the band or orchestra will play.

Billboard The tag or logo at the end of a commercial.

Board *See* console.

Bouncing Combining several tracks onto one track so that the resulting empty tracks can be used to record other material.

Click Track A metronome that is calibrated at a number of beats per frames of film. It is used to maintain a precise tempo.

Composer A musician who writes original music.

Console The main control panel that regulates all the sounds of the tape recorder(s) in a recording studio.

Conversion Chart A chart that converts feet of film to seconds and minutes and visa versa.

Demo A sample tape used by announcers, actors, singers, music houses, etc.

Direct Recording Recording an electric instrument directly to the tape recorder (via the console) without the use of an amplifier.

Donut A "hole" in a commercial where announcer copy is inserted.

Doubling *See* multing.

Drop-In A pre-existing music track into which your product name is inserted.

Dub A tape copy.

Dubber A machine that plays full coats and stripes, found in a film-mix facility.

Echo A sound enhancement system that gives the illusion of having recorded the material in a large room or hall.

EQ *See* equalizer.

Equalizer A sophisticated tone control devise on the recording console.

Fader A movable, sliding switch that regulates the volume of each track on the console.

Flat Recording Recording without echo or equalization.

Full Coat A 35mm piece of film "fully coated" with oxide that contains three separate tracks of audio information. (See insert inside front cover.)

Full-lyric Version   The original version of the commercial with a complete lyric.

Full-track Tape Recorder   A monaural tape recorder.

Half-track Tape Recorder   A two-track tape recorder (stereo) that is not compatible with home stereo tape systems.

IPS   Inches Per Second. Refers to the speed of the tape.

Kem   A table-top type of film editing machine.

Leakage   Occurs when material recorded on one microphone leaks over to another microphone.

Level   The amount of signal either going to the tape recorder or being returned during playback.

Library Music   Prerecorded music classified by tempo and mood, usually available on records.

Lip-sync   When the actor or actresses' lip movements are in sync with the sound track.

Looping   A technique for repeating a portion of film over and over while an actor or announcer records the spoken part.

Mag   A "magnetic transfer." Refers to either a full coat or a stripe.

Master   The final finished mix.

Mix   *See* Mixdown.

Mixdown   Reducing a multi-track recording to either a mono or stereo tape.

Monaural   One track.

Monitor   The part of the studio console used for playback of a tape.

Movieola   The most popular machine used for editing and assembling film.

Multing   Repeating vocal parts on additional tracks to create the illusion of a larger group.

Multi-track Recorder   A studio tape recorder designed to record separately on 4, 8, 16, 24, or 32 tracks.

Music House   An independent production company that writes music for commercials, TV, and feature films.

Needle Drop   Each use of library music in a commercial.

Noise Reduction   A system for reducing tape hiss. DBX and Dolby are the most common systems in use.

Overdubbing   Adding parts on top of an existing tape. Also referred to as sel-syncing.

Pan   The process by which you place an instrument to the left, right, center—or anywhere—during a stereo mix.

Pilotone   A special type of sync signal encoded onto a tape, used to keep the tape recorder in sync with the camera when shooting a commercial.

Post-scoring   Recording the music or audio track after shooting the commercial.

Pre-production   The preparation and planning that takes place before a commercial is actually shot or recorded.

Pre-scoring   Recording the music or audio track before shooting the commercial.

Punching   Re-recording a portion of a taped performance.

Quarter-track Tape Recorder   The consumer version of a professional half-track tape recorder.

Recording Console   *See* Console.

Recording Tape   Refers to ¼-inch, ½-inch, 1-inch or 2-inch tape used on a tape recorder. (See insert inside front cover.)

Residuals   Re-use fees paid to talent for the on-air use of a commercial.

Resolver   A machine that reads and interprets a sync signal encoded on a tape and then keeps that tape running at a constant speed.

SAG   Screen Actors Guild. The union that governs the payments to singers, actors, announcers, and models appearing in *filmed* commercials, as opposed to radio or videotape. The sister union to AFTRA.

Scale   The minimum payments for recording sessions and film shoots as determined by AFM, AFTRA, and SAG.

Sel-sync   (sel-synchronization) A term used to describe the process during which the record head of a tape recorder temporarily acts as a playback head. This makes overdubbing and bouncing possible.

Signatory   A person or company that agrees to abide by the union agreements set by the talent unions.

Spot   A radio or TV commercial.

Stereo   Two-channel recordings containing separate information for the left and right speakers.

Stripe   A monaural mag. The stripe actually has two stripes. The second is referred to as a "balance stripe," which keeps this type of mag evenly wound on its hub. (See sample insert inside front cover.)

Studio Console   *See* Console.

Sync Signal   A 60-cycle signal that is encoded on the tape at the original recording session. When read by a resolver, sync signal keeps the tape running at a given speed.

Tag   *See* billboard.

Tracks   Separate linear sections that run parallel to each other on recording tape, as in "24-tracks."

Two-track   *See* half-track.

Voiceover   Spoken words recited by an actor or announcer for a commercial.

A Dictionary of Contemporary Musical Styles

It is our intention to list styles by category, so that you can have a better grasp of the kaleidoscope of musical styles available today. We have tried to list artists whose records are readily available for you to purchase for reference and who are played often on the radio.

Blues

Big Band Blues	Joe Williams
Chicago Blues	Muddy Waters
Delta Blues	Robert Johnson
Modern—eclectic	Ry Cooder
Modern—electric	B.B. King
Soul	Ray Charles, Aretha Franklin, Curtis Mayfield, Smokey Robinson

Broadway

Broadway Shows	*A Chorus Line, Annie*
Off-Broadway Shows	*The Fantasticks, Scrambled Feet*
Revues	*Ain't Misbehavin', Sophisticated Ladies*

Country & Western (C & W)

Bluegrass	Bill Monroe, Lester Flatt & Earl Scruggs
Cajun	Doug Kershaw
Country Pop	Dolly Parton, Ronnie Milsap, Emmylou Harris
Country Rock	Billy Swann, Roy Orbison
Instrumental	Chet Atkins, Jerry Reed
Mainstream	Johnny Cash
Newgrass	The Newgrass Revival
Outlaw	Waylon Jennings, Willie Nelson
Singer-Songwriter	Kris Kristofferson, Johnny Cash
Texas Swing	Bob Wills and the Texas Playboys

Tex-Mex   Marty Robbins, Johnny Rodroguez
Traditional   Hank Snow, Ernest Tubb
Truck Driver   Dave Dudley
Western   Gene Autry, Sons of the Pioneers

Folk

Ballads   Burl Ives
Folk Rock   The Byrds
Instrumental   Doc Watson, John Renbourn
Mainstream   Pete Seeger
Pop Folk   Peter, Paul & Mary, The Kingston Trio
Protest   Woody Guthrie, Arlo Guthrie
Singer-Songwriter   Tom Paxton, early Joni Mitchell

Hollywood

General   *Star Wars, Jaws*
Original Cast   *Saturday Night Fever, The Last Waltz,*
                           The Rose

Jazz

Bebop   Charlie Parker, Dizzy Gillespie, Lambert,
                           Hendricks & Ross
Big Band   Count Basie, Woody Herman
Bossa Nova   Joao Gilberto, Charlie Byrd
Dixieland   Louis Armstrong
Fusion   Herbie Hancock, Chick Corea, Bob
                           James
Latin   Tito Puente, Cal Tjader
Mainstream   Roy Eldridge, Buck Clayton
Post Bebop   John Coltrane
Swing   Benny Goodman
Third Stream   Anthony Braxton, Cecil Taylor
    (avant garde)
Vocal   Lambert, Hendricks & Ross

Pop (Middle of the Road—MOR)

Instrumental   Lawrence Welk, Percy Faith, Ray
                           Conniff

Vocal Groups	Johnny Mann Singers, Ray Charles Singers, Percy Faith, Carpenters
Vocal Soloists	Frank Sinatra, Tony Bennett, Carole King, Karen Carpenter

Religious

Christian Rock	Andrea Crouch & the Disciples
Gospel Groups (black)	Dixie Hummingbirds, The Five Blind Boys
Gospel Groups (white)	The Rambos
Gospel Soloists (black)	Reverend James Cleveland, Mahalia Jackson
Gospel Soloists (white)	Reba Rambo
Gospel Pop	The Oak Ridge Boys
Gospel Rock	The Mighty Clouds of Joy

Rock and Roll (Rock)

Blues	Rolling Stones
Country Rock	Emmylou Harris, Dolly Parton
Disco	Donna Summers, Sister Sledge, Stephanie Mills
Fifties Rock (Soloists)	Chuck Berry, Little Richard
Fifties Rock (Groups)	The Shangrilas, The Coasters
Folk Rock	The Byrds
Glitter Rock	David Bowie
Heavy Metal	Led Zeppelin, Black Sabbath, Blue Oyster Cult
Jazz Rock	Chicago, Blood Sweat & Tears
Mainstream	The Beatles
Pop Rock	Barry Manilow, Abba
New Wave	Blondie
Punk	The Police, The Pretenders, Joe Jackson, Elvis Costello, Tom Petty and the Heartbreakers
Singer-Songwriter	Jackson Browne, Carly Simon, James Taylor, Paul Simon
Vocal Groups	Bee Gees, The Beach Boys, Crosby Stills Nash & Young

Bibliography

This bibliography is intended as a guide to auxiliary readings that the authors have found useful to their own thought processes. We have omitted the standard business texts, and the "How I Made It in Advertising" memoirs, which we assume you will readily encounter.

Anderton, Craig. *Home Recording for Musicians*. New York: Guitar Player Books, 1978. A guide to studio design and use for the professional musician. This book is oriented to the musician who wants to build a small home studio.

Beck, Albert C., and Cary, Norman D. *The Radio and Television Commercial*. Chicago: Crain Books, 1978. A comprehensive and useful guide to radio and television commercials.

Dolan, Robert Emmett. *Music in Modern Media*. New York: G. Schirmer, 1967. This is a good book, but a bit dated.

Eargle, John M. *Sound Recording*. New York: Van Nostrand Reinhold, 1976. A detailed discussion.

Fredricks, Mark. *The Use of Click Track for Radio and TV Commercials*. New York: Comprehensive Publications Inc., 1974. Mark Fredricks is the music producer for BBD&O in New York City. This is an excellent book on click and the only one to include 16mm film.

Hopkins, Claude. *Scientific Advertising*. New York: Chelsea House, 1980. Originally published in 1923, this is one of the classic discussions of the theory and practice of advertising.

Karmen, Steve. *The Jingle Man*. Winona, Minn.: 1980. Words and music to many famous jingles of a top New York composer.

Knudson, Carroll. *Project Tempo, Volumes I & II*. Los Angeles: Valley Publishing, 1965. For 35mm and videotape, these are the best click books available.

Lipton, Lenny. *Independent Film Making*. New York: Simon & Schuster, Fireside Books, 1972. A complete guide to the film process, including the use of sound. Not for the casual reader.

Lustig, Milton. *Music Editing for Motion Pictures*. New York: Hastings House, 1980. For those who want to delve deeper into this area.

Martineau, Pierre. *Motivation in Advertising: Motives That Make People Buy*. New York: McGraw-Hill, 1957, paperback ed., 1971.

McLuhan, Marshall. *Understanding Media*. New York: McGraw-Hill, 1964. A classic.

Nisbett, Alec. *The Techniques of the Sound Studio*. 4th ed. New York, Hastings House, 1979. An authoritative and lengthy explanation of recording studio procedures.

Norback, Peter, and Norback, Craig, Eds. *Great Songs of Madison Avenue*. New

York: Quadrangle/The New York Times Book Co., 1976. Lots of your favorite jingles from Pepsi-Cola to Pan Am. The complete words and music.

Price, Jonathan. *The Best Thing on TV: Commercials*. New York: Penguin Books, 1978. An amusing if somewhat over-awed study of the making and execution of commercials.

Roman, Kenneth, and Maas, Jane. *How to Advertise*. New York: St. Martin's Press, 1976.

Runstein, Robert. *Modern Recording Techniques*. Indianapolis: Howard W. Sams, 1969.

Schrank, Jeffrey. *Snap, Crackle and Popular Taste: The Illusion of Free Choice in America*. New York: Delta Books, 1977. If you find yourself falling in love with advertising, this book may break up the romance.

Schwartz, Tony. *The Responsive Chord*. New York: Anchor Books, 1973. Techniques of persuasion and communication.

Seiden, Hank. *Advertising Pure and Simple*. New York: Anacom, 1976.

Teixeira, Antonio, Jr. *Music to Sell By*. Boston: Berklee Press, 1974. This book is intended for musicians and composers who want to learn the craft of writing music for commercials.

Wainwright, Charles Anthony. *Television Commercials: How to Create Successful TV Advertising*. New York: Hastings House, 1977.

Weissman, Dick. *The Music Business: Career Opportunities and Self-Defense*. New York: Crown, 1979. A general guide to the music business with a chapter on commercials.

Wright, John, ed. *The Commercial Connection: Advertising and the American Mass Media*. New York: Delta Books, 1979. A useful collection of articles discussing various aspects of advertising and the media.

Directories

Sound Effects Records   Catalog available from Thomas J. Valentino, 151 W. 46th St. New York 10036 "Major Records."

The Creative Black Book   An invaluable source book for the advertising industry. Friendly Publications, New York, NY

Backstage Directory   Another invaluable reference book, issued annually for the advertising industry. Backstage Publications, New York, NY

Motion Picture, TV and Theatre Directory   A general purpose hand guide to both the motion picture and advertising industry. Motion Picture Enterprises, Inc.; Tarrytown, New York 10591.

INDEX